ORIENTAL MYSTICISM

Oriental Mysticism

by
Edward Stevens

PAULIST PRESS
New York / Paramus / Toronto

Library of Congress
Catalog Card Number: 73-87030

ISBN 0-8091-1798-3

Published by Paulist Press
Editorial Office: 1865 Broadway, N.Y., N.Y. 10023
Business Office: 400 Sette Drive, Paramus, N.J. 07652

Printed and bound in the
United States of America

Contents

To
Mother and Dad

"Thank you for your life!"

Introduction

Books on mysticism can be grouped into three classes:

(1) the mainly *psychological*, e.g., Naranjo and Ornstein, *On the Psychology of Meditation* (Esalen Books, 1971); Johnston, *The Still Point* (Fordham, 1970); Pearce, *The Crack in the Cosmic Egg* (Julian, 1971); Johansson, *The Psychology of Nirvana* (Anchor, 1970);

(2) the predominantly *philosophical-theological*, e.g., Toulmin, *The Oriental Philosophers* (Harper, 1963); Smart, *Doctrine and Argument in Indian Philosophy* (Unwin, 1964); Zaehner, *Indian and Muslim Mysticism* (Schocken, 1969);

(3) the mainly *devotional*, e.g., Néodoncelle's *God's Encounter with Man* (Burns and Oates, 1964), and countless pop and popular books of every religious persuasion. Happold's *Mysticism* (Pelican, 1967) and Suzuki's *Mysticism: Christian and Buddhist* are devotional-philosophical in approach.

What is hard to find is an integrated treatment which combines the experience, theory and practice of mysticism. The psychological approach alone treats mysticism as if it could occur in a cultural vacuum. It neglects the peculiar texture that various philosophical orientations lend to the experience. The philosophical treatment alone leaves the subject detached from both psychological experience and technical practice. The devotional treatments tend to be narrowly confessional, missing the variety and richness that psychological and philosophical contexts provide, and thus limiting even the level of devotional practice. This book attempts in a non-technical way to combine psychology, philosophy and practice. The philosophies, however, will be confined to the oriental mystical traditions of India, China, and Japan.

A short first chapter leads the reader to the practice of mysticism. The next three chapters define the core of qualities common to experiences called mystical. Three paths to mystical experience are described: the outward path of concentration and absorption, the inward path of surrender and self-expression, and the negative path of detachment. The second part of the book is devoted to the various oriental interpretations of mystical experience. We will look first at two branches of Hinduism, *Vedanta* and *Sankhya-Yoga*. Then, successive chapters will treat Buddhism, Chinese Taoism, and Japanese Zen. The final chapter deals in the light of modern psychology with objections brought against the practice of mysticism.

Thanks are due to Canisius College for the Faculty Fellowship Grant which supported the writing of this book.

One final note. I have not succeeded, or even tried, to acknowledge all the sources that have influenced the ideas in this book. Though filtered through my own experience, they are not original. The most recent and immediate references I used are cited in the footnotes. I refer the reader to those books for a deeper understanding of what I treat in a summarized and introductory way.

ORIENTAL MYSTICISM

SWAMI SATCHIDANANDA—FOUNDER OF INTEGRAL YOGA IN-
STITUTE.
Photo by Ivan Spane.

I
How To Meditate

(From the files of an unknown guru)

1/24/52
My Pet Lizard Died a Year Ago Today!
Hello, Mystic Master.

I'm the crazy lady with the green shawl you met last week. I was in the front row of the lecture hall, remember? I was thrilled by your talk on mysticism. Could you give me lessons? I could come in for instruction any day at any time you say. And I can pay or make a generous offering for your work.

Please write me, Mystic Master. Give me some advice on prayer, a program to follow, books to read. I want to learn from you. Write me soon, won't you?

The Crazy Lady

Sunrise
My Dear Crazy Lady,

I have nothing more to say to you about prayer. Let me talk to you instead about your pet lizard.

To have a lizard as a friend requires long grooming, much talking and feeding. You can train a dog, but a lizard has to be seduced.

Dogs and human beings permit themselves to be fitted into slots. You can teach them tricks. They can be manipulated like puppets. Better still, after a while you don't even have to pull the puppet strings. They will obediently jerk their limbs in the grotesque and ungainly gestures you taught them.

A lizard won't do tricks for you. A lizard is too much in touch with the secret source of his lizard life. It is too precious to give away. A lizard will slither and scurry as lizards are born to do. And a lizard knows whom he can trust: he knows who will respect his lizard ways. He stays far from the man who would have him jump and beg and roll over on command.

But if you train them right, dogs will walk on their hind legs, and humans will beg on all fours. Dogs and human beings easily learn to forget their own secret source of life. They lose their original innocence. It's like the towering primaeval grandeur of the giant redwood tree reaching for the heavens. Cut it down. Fashion the wood into tables and chairs. What's left of the tree? Tables and chairs, scraps and shavings. What do these have in common? Both the furniture and the scraps have lost their original redwood innocence. The respectable citizen is more respectable than the robber. But they agree in this: both have lost their original innocence. As the Hindu saying goes, "A nightingale in a golden cage is no freer than one in a cage of iron."

And so, Crazy Lady, you want to recover your lost innocence. You want me to teach you how to meditate. Your lizard was the best teacher you ever had. With you, I lament his passing. Make friends with another, patiently, respectfully. Pay attention to him. Be still. Watch. And learn. Nothing could be more important for you, Crazy Lady. Start today.

The Mystic Master

For your information, reader, the following is the text of The Mystic Master's lecture which so enthused

The Crazy Lady. I include it here because meditation is a matter of practice rather than theory. When you get to the solemn theories later in the book, you'll have a better chance of tuning into them if you're practicing meditation on your own.

The Lecture

I have come to talk to you about mysticism, or prayer, or meditation—whatever you prefer to call it. It is a theme of works as diverse as the Esalen publication, *On the Psychology of Meditation,*[1] Catholic Néodoncelle's *God's Encounter with Man: A Contemporary Approach to Prayer,*[2] or Joan Baez's autobiography, *Daybreak.*[3]

Our drug culture has preached new levels of awareness through hallucinogens (i.e., hallucination-producing drugs) like LSD and mescaline or the milder marijuana, and through the "up" and "down" drugs of the straight world, amphetamines and barbiturates. But chemicals are not the only key to expanded consciousness. The Buddha, Jesus, Gandhi, Oriental and Occidental monks, poets and reflective work-a-day people have practiced the path of quiet meditation. Call it Buddhist *satori*, or Hindu cosmic consciousness, call it Christian mystical union, or aesthetic transcendental experience. Or use the current slang and call it "turning on without drugs."

We'll answer two questions: What's it mean to be "turned off"? How do you go about "turning on"?

It is a fact that most of us operate on one psychic cylinder. The best part of our minds is turned off. We live in what biochemist Robert de Ropp calls "waking sleep." Our eyes are open, we move around. We appear to be awake, but the highest and best part of ourselves is sound asleep. "Buddha" in Sanskrit means "Awakened One." We are non-Buddhas. We are unawakened. The unawakened man is like a puppet. He doesn't live life, but lets life live him. He has literally lost his mind.

Not the inner self, but outside strings control this puppet. His three-year-old whines, and he automatically roars back. The doorbell rings, the puppet jumps. The boss raises an eyebrow, the puppet sulks. His wife needles him, he jabs right back. A referee whistles a foul, a signal for the puppet to boo. A red traffic light triggers a curse. While eating with his family, his mind is at the office. His body goes to bed, but his thoughts are with tomorrow's customers. He couldn't tell you what he had for breakfast or read in the newspaper five minutes afterward.

The mind and the limbs of the puppet's wife are equally wooden. They move jerkily to the pulling of strings: to a ringing phone and the chime of an oven timer, to bills and color-filled ads, to insufferable in-laws and long-haired neighborhood kids. Her mind is absent from the scene. She centers on the Ohrbach dress, the private school, the blue Volkswagen they cannot afford, the party she wasn't invited to and the vacation her children got sick for.

To sum up, in waking sleep we don't know who we are, what we're doing, or why we're doing it. We are the plaything of the sights and sounds and people around us, but we don't really hear or see them. The present moment is all we have, but the present passes us by, while future and past join to pull our minds apart.

This doesn't have to be so. We can wake up that best

part of the mind which puts us in tune and turns us on. A college junior did, and told me: "I just sit quietly, and gradually I get in tune with myself inside and my senses are in rhythm with the world outside. My ears pick out the individual sounds around me. Colors seem brilliant, unique. People appear newborn as if I had never seen them before. I want to laugh. Everything is so funny, and alive, and beautiful. I'm turned on. I'm living *now*."

A housewife put it this way: "I perch on a stool in the kitchen and pay attention. The hum of the electric clock on the wall mixes with the traffic rumbling down Main Street. Angry thoughts pop into my mind, and worries about how to pay for a new dress. I get an urge to get up and wash my stockings or light a cigarette. But I do nothing, just sit quietly and observe. Gradually my mind unwinds, and I feel peace. I'm ready to face the world again, stronger and more secure. I'm in tune with myself and everything."

And from an insurance salesman: "Before a tough sale, I spend time alone, and utterly quiet. My anxiety slides away, and somehow a power comes up from inside of me, and I am master of myself again. And like radar, I pick up not only what my client says, but what he feels and doesn't say. I'm plugged in to myself and everything going on around me."

"I'd sooner go through life with my eyes closed than let the din of everyday living drown out my higher mind," an artist confessed to me.

How can *you* turn on these powers, expand *your* consciousness?

Like a muscle weak with disuse, your higher mind needs daily exercise to become active again, or for the first time. Take a few minutes a day to gradually dis-

cover your higher powers and eventually to bring them
to full flower. Let's call this daily exercise meditation.
It involves the body, the mind, and the senses.

First, the body. Find a place where you will not be
disturbed for five to fifteen minutes. It doesn't have to
be quiet as long as no one can break in and interrupt
you. You manage to find fifteen uninterrupted minutes
for coffee or an errand. Surely you can find a quarter
of an hour for your best investment, your own self.
Adopt a relaxed but alert position. A Hindu yogi might
sit in the cross-legged "lotus" position. A Christian
monk might kneel. But these unaccustomed positions
are too uncomfortable for most of us. Try sitting with
your hands on your lap, but not leaning your back
against anything. You want to be comfortable, but also
alert and still, absolutely still: a rare experience for
most of the waking sleepers. We are either alert and
agitated or asleep and still, but seldom are we alert and
also still.

Now, for the mind. At first it will be running wildly
at top speed, telling you all the things you could be
doing better than just sitting still, or unreeling a thousand images of yesterday's regrets and triumphs. That's
all right! Relax. Watch your thoughts run. They might
get embarrassed and slow down! Benedictine monk
Dom Aelred Graham[4] suggests the ideal:

Living in the present is to keep one's mind like a mirror, unsmudged by hopes or fears, anticipations or regrets, so that one sees precisely what one looks at and
judges only what one sees.

Such is the awakened mind.

Some people have a *mantra* (Sanskrit for "a sacred
word or phrase"), a phrase they repeat with each breath

so that the rhythmic breathing with the regular repetition gradually brings the mind to peace. A well-known Buddhist *mantra* is *aum mane padme hum* (the words signify the state of the universe moving from many parts to a single unity—just as your meditation moves you from a bundle of distractions to a unity with your highest self). Breathe out as you recite *aum mane;* breathe in as you say *padme hum.* If you prefer a Christian *mantra,* you could repeat in the same rhythmic way a favorite phrase from the "Lord's Prayer" (e.g., "Our Father," or perhaps "Give us this day," or "Thy will be done"). The poet Tennyson's *mantra* was the rhythmic repetition of his own name! Hear him tell it:

A kind of waking trance I have frequently had, quite up from boyhood, when I have been all alone. This has generally come upon me thro' repeating my own name two or three times to myself silently, till all at once, as it were out of the intensity of the consciousness of individuality, the individuality itself seems to dissolve and fade away into boundless being, and this is not a confused state but the clearest, the surest of the surest.[5]

Such is the awakened mind.

Now, for the senses. As your mind and body become still, your senses should be paying attention to the tastes and fragrances peculiar to this very room, to the breezes and temperatures, pressures and caresses that seduce the quietly alert radar of your skin and touch, to the moan of a passing jet punctuated by a backfiring truck, to the hum of your refrigerator signaling its work along with your gently hissing stove. You might feel that your house and everything in it are alive, and glad you noticed! Folk singer Joan Baez describes her meditation this way:

To pay attention, but not to concentrate, to be still, and at the same time to let go. To stop rehearsing, stop the fantasies. Look with your eyes. I don't know what there is to see. Listen with your ears. Everything is alive. Perhaps you can hear it being alive. Sit there. . . . By missing the minute, you are missing everything, because all you have is that minute.[6]

Such is the awakened mind.

That's it: (1) a space and time when you can be undisturbed; (2) a posture that is relaxed and alert; (3) a mind which lets go, and watches itself slow down; (4) eyes that see, ears that hear, and a taste and touch which register every vibration. A little Zen poem sums it up:

Sitting quietly, doing nothing,
spring comes, and the grass grows by itself.

Your higher mind will awaken by itself.

How long to meditate? For waking sleepers, quiet meditation is the hardest exercise in the world. Try five minutes a day at first, then ten, fifteen—as long as possible. Hindu monks have extended this exercise for days!

And a warning: Don't expect anything. Don't try for special effects. Just wait and see what happens. Expanded consciousness can't be forced. Give it a chance, and it comes of its own accord.

If exercised regularly, your expanded consciousness will be part not only of your moments of meditation but increasingly of your life as well. You will walk the world with the waking sleepers, but *you* will not be asleep. You will know who you are. When you act, you will know what you are doing and why. You will not react to sights, but you will really see. You will not walk deaf and distracted, but will listen and respond to the beckonings of life around you. The present moment which is all you have will be your focus. You will become sensitive to your heart's deepest promptings, and these will be your guide. All of your senses will truly be in tune with the pulsing world in which you move.

Turn on without drugs. Meditation, after all, is cheaper than drugs. It's legal! And it's safer and always available. There is a higher consciousness in you, asleep, perhaps. Give it a chance to wake up. Become a Buddha, an "Awakened One."

SRI CHINMOY—INDIAN SPIRITUAL MASTER, LEADING MEDITATION AT ST. PAUL'S CHAPEL, COLUMBIA UNIVERSITY.

Photo by Ivan Spane.

II
Concentrative Meditation

Today I look at the world through dreary blue glasses. Yesterday my emotional tint was bright yellow. Tomorrow, I hope it will be a soothing green.

It's Monday—a working day. No nonsense, no lying in bed. Keep an eye on the clock. No lounging about with magazines. TV set off. I've got a job to do, and so much time to do it in. Filter out every distraction.

I'm a city boy, myself. Trucks and cabs, Fords and Chevies go roaring by my window. I don't hear them. The ventilator hums. My watch ticks. Both go unheeded and unheard. I couldn't tell you the last song played on the radio. I have ears only for the time checks. All else is filtered out.

I'm an American. There was a train wreck in Zaire, yesterday, a fire in Bangladesh, and a new mayor in Guayaquil. This news is fit to print and you'll find it in the *Times*. But give me the local paper. I'm much more concerned about the local sales tax and last night's score of the home team. The rest I filter out.

Filter on filter on filter between me and the world. I go about inside an insulated bubble. One-half of one percent of the light gets through. I don't want to see the rest. I'm a one-watt bulb. I'm ninety-nine percent unconscious.

Mysticism is the art of becoming fully conscious. It is the way of removing the filters. It is the path to getting fully in tune with reality. Mysticism is a new way

of being that transforms everything it touches. It puts
me in touch with my deepest self, my hidden powers.
So profoundly does it transform me that the mystic
state is described as touching the divine.

There are three types of meditation, three ways of
moving from the conditioned filtered world of The
Known to that mysterious fullness of The Unknown.
There is the outer directed formal path of concentration. There is the inner directed spontaneous path of
surrender. And, third, there is the negative path of detachment and self-emptying. We will consider these
three mystical paths in turn, starting in this chapter
with the path of concentration.

It is not easy to talk about meditation. We are looking to become conscious in a way that is unknown to
our ordinary everyday minds. And for the unknown, we
have no words. That's why practice is so important.
Indeed, it is everything. A. J. Muste has said: "There is
no way to peace; peace is the way." So we might say:
"There is no way to meditation; meditation is the
way."

In concentrative meditation, the focus is outside of
myself. I put myself in the presence of The Other, call
it God, or Reality, or The Buddha, or the risen Christ.
Like a lover in the presence of his beloved, I sit silently
in the presence of the Unknown.

What do I do? How do I get in touch with a Mystery
I know nothing about? I concentrate on a *symbol* of
this Unknown Presence. I concentrate on an object
which represents the Other. The act of absorbing myself in the sign is the beginning of my actual union with
the Other. The goal doesn't come at the end, like pay-
day. No. To begin to concentrate is to begin to live the
new life.

The object of concentration can be visual, a crucifix, the sun, a flame, the lotus. It can be verbal, one of the names of God, a short prayer, an aspiration such as "peace" or "love." It can be aural, such as a bell or a drum. It can be a combination, such as a rising stream of incense, which is an object of both sight and smell.

These images exert their own power over me. I give myself to them, and they take over. Without thinking or analyzing, I just gaze or listen. The traditional images used in concentrative meditation accomplish three things in me. They draw me to the center of Reality. They invite me to self-emptying surrender. And they put me in tune with the law and pattern of the universe. Let's consider them in turn—centering, surrender, and universal order.

First, centering. For example, I focus on a flame of a candle or on the sun itself. (Sun-gazing, eyelids half lowered, is widely practiced in India; each morning the beaches and public parks are dotted with people sitting rapt in solar concentration.) And I get a sense of all energy flowing from a single source. By conforming to an external unifying image I get in touch with the center of unity in myself. The sun or the flame is the outer sign of the interior inner state which meditation brings about. It is an efficacious sign, a sacrament. It brings about that which it signifies. Centuries of experience attest to the power of these universal meditation symbols. As the sun's and the flame's energy and light flow from a central radiating source, so I come to experience the energy and light that flow from the depths of my own center that I so seldom visit.

Verbal images such as the name of God have this same centering power. Repeated rhythmically over and over again, the name of "Jesus," the Sacred Hindu syllable "OM," the invocation "Our Father," the "Hare Krishna" mantra, recall me to the divine center of unity outside of me which is at the same time the deep inner source of my own being and unity.

Besides their "centering" power, these universal images are sacraments (i.e., efficacious signs) of the meditative state of self-surrender. In my ordinary consciousness, I cling anxiously to my desires, satisfactions, and self-centered needs. Concentration on the crucifix transforms this ego-centered consciousness. I come to sense the life that comes from death and self-surrender. It is not a matter of reasoning. It is rather a matter of giving myself over to the presence and power symbolized by the crucifix. Such too is the understanding conveyed by the flame, its light and life born in the very consuming of the candle. Such, too, is the lotus, whose seed must die that the bloom may flower forth.

Finally, concentrative meditation not only finds in the Other a source of centeredness and surrender, but also discovers there the source of harmony and order. And so concentration focuses on words like "Thy will be done," or on the cross where opposite polarities intersect in the center—a reconciliation of yin and yang. Too, the Tibetan mandala symbolizes this universal order. And so the meditator concentrates on the mandala design, a regular pattern which comes to a point in the center, symbolic of the law of the universe where the one and the many are reconciled. Each great mystical tradition teaches a path to universal regularity. Thus the Hindu seeks union with *Brahman*. The Buddhist lives his *Bharma*. And in China, harmony is the *Tao*, the universal Way.

Centeredness, self-surrender, harmony—such is the transformed awareness of the meditative state. To be aware *is* to receive. There is no way to centeredness, self-surrender, and harmony. Rather centeredness, self-surrender, and harmony are themselves the way. Concentrative meditation is itself the goal, is its own reward. Be still. Recall Chuang-Tzu:[1] "Heaven acts on all things, but meddles in none." I must become still, ready myself, if Heaven is to act. To talk about meditation is easy. The cultural trappings of crosses and mandalas, incense and mantras, are easily described and passed on. But the experience itself is utterly personal. The former can flourish while the latter dies out. Flourishing trade in psychedelic paraphernalia need not signal the widespread practice of concentrative meditation. The active fight to survive—dog eat dog—is our biggest illusion. I need not grasp the Other. I need only be still, allow the Other to grasp me. It is by willingness to risk death that I gain life.

Death, passivity, emptiness—how can these be real human ideals? How can you ask me to stand by passively in the face of human misery, suffering, and poverty? The Oriental may view this world as a great illusion, but for me the world is real, pain is harsh, suffering and poverty are to be actively fought, not passively tolerated. Aren't you proposing a new form of the old opium? Pie in the sky won't feed me here on earth.

Not so. It is not a question of passivity *or* activity, death *or* life, emptiness *or* fullness. The old is always a particular example of the new and wider view. Einstein's theory did not abolish Newton's laws but incorporated them from a higher point of view. We could even say that Darwin's evolutionary hypothesis did not abolish the Genesis creation story but set it into a more comprehensive context. Genesis was weak on measuring time, but it had the *order* of creation (evolution) just about right! Mysticism does not deny life, fullness, and activity, but leads me to live more fully and actively than ever from a consciousness that is now transformed. Equanimity is not the enemy of love nor does emptiness negate compassion. A man who is mystically transformed is more widely active and compassionate than he was before.

It is sacrifice that symbolizes this paradox and brings it into focus. Unfortunately, in the Western humanist world, the notion of sacrifice repels. It appears as a sign of destruction. Life is sacred. Sacrifice spills blood, destroys life. What kind of sadistic God would exact the death of his own son to atone for sin as the Christian tradition recounts? Doesn't this strike as more vicious than even human sacrifice? To what point is the spilling of animal blood? When sacrifice signifies divine sadism, it is vicious indeed. When sacrifice seems an invitation to masochism, I am rightly repelled. In view of these perverted distortions even Roman Christianity has begun to play down the sacrificial dimension of its Eucharistic rite, and not without cost. But in evading the distortion, the healthy life-giving function of sacrifice has been lost as well.

As the flame, the sun, and the name of God are outer images of my inner identity, so sacrifice is the outer image of the love and compassion that are born from equanimity and emptiness. Consider. What do I sacrifice? Not activity, but the walls that dam up my activity. Not love, but the egoism which makes loving impossible. Not compassion, but selfishness that hardens the heart. This is the meaning symbolized by the animal sacrifices of the Hindu *Vedas*,[2] the human sacrifices of the Aztecs, and the God-sacrifice in Christianity reenacted in the Eucharist. These rituals can become empty magical external rites. But when the worshiper by concentrative meditation permits their meaning to take hold of him, then, transformed, he lives on a higher level. Giving is not a draining, but an exercise of power. Emptiness is not a vacuum, but a freedom to become filled. Equanimity is not indifference, but the liberty to show compassion and the sensitivity to notice the misery which invites compassion in whatever form that misery appears.

There is a further paradox about the meditative state. Meditation is, on the one hand, a discovery of my oneness with Reality. Yet, at the same time, it appears as a religious confrontation with an "Other" that transcends me. Unity and duality, oneness and distinction—let's consider in turn each side of this paradox.

First, unity. Through concentration, the meditator becomes one with the object of meditation and with the reality symbolized by it. Concentration is not like the regular thinking process in which I solve problems by distinguishing and classifying objects, separating subjective knowing and objective known, and drawing conclusions. Meditation seeks no *useful* purpose. The world of utility and pragmatic everyday living is precisely the world which meditation moves beyond. Where thinking begets distinctions, loving concentration brings unity. I become so absorbed by the object that I do not exist for myself anymore but the object fills me. That is why it is so terribly important whom and what I love, whom and what I allow to absorb me. I become what I love. I can allow myself to be absorbed by money or alcohol, or by the divine.

Concentration, then, is a movement out of the world of pragmatism and distinctions into the world of absorption and unity. Ordinary utilitarian consciousness becomes transformed unitary consciousness. I break out of the cage where habit has put me. Ordinary labels break down; right and wrong, I and you, self and world no longer fit in rigidly separate boxes.

The Chinese teach their children a game to break them out of the cage of ordinary thinking. It's called the "pillow" game. Suppose two children quarrel. How do they resolve their differences? Each sits down opposite the other, with a square pillow between them. A problem, like a pillow, has four sides and a center. The child places his folded hands on side one of the pillow and says, "There is a place where I am right and you are wrong." Then he shifts his hands to side two, saying, "There is another place where you are right and I am wrong." Moving to side three, he says, "There is also a place where we are at the same time both right and both wrong." Next, placing his hands on side four, he says, "And there is a place where neither of us is either right or wrong and the whole thing can be forgotten." Finally, cupping his hands in the center of the pillow, the child affirms "There is a center from which all these approaches flow." At the center, the child, as it were, holds the whole problem in his hands. Then moving back from four, to three, two, and one, the child asserts: "Each one of these steps is good." By using this technique, the child does not stay trapped in the narrow one-dimensional world of either-or, right or wrong, black or white. It is to just such a world, beyond ordinary distinctions, that the meditative state leads us. By concentrative meditation we live at that unnamed unified center from which all four viewpoints flow. There is a beautiful freedom in living at the center. The child gets up from the pillow game relieved from the need to win (step one), or the fear of losing (step two). He knows other possibilities. He can admit to being partly right and partly wrong (step three). He can even laugh as the whole problem vanishes (step four). After all, he is the center from which all these approaches emanate. Life at the center—this is an apt description of the meditative state.

Unity, life at the center—I become my deepest true self, I become the universe, I become, in a sense, "God." But is this sufficient to describe the meditative state? Our descriptions so far have been purely psychological and naturalistic, a mysticism without "God." Mysticism certainly can be viewed on the one level of purely human psychology. But is it sufficient to view the mystical state in this one-dimensional way? Is the mystical state a phenomenon which is religious as well as psychological? Do I not only *become* "God" but in a sense reach out for, Encounter, and *confront* "God"? Is mysticism a state of worship as well as a state of mind? Is a call to immanence at once a call to transcendence?

Clearly, the great mystical traditions discuss the mystical state in terms of duality, worship, and religion as well as of unity, consciousness and psychology. Along with the natural dimension, a second or "supernatural" dimension is felt to be involved. Not all of the traditions speak of "God." Later on in the book, we will discuss the various religious-philosophical categories used by Hinduism, Buddhism, Taoism, and Zen to interpret mystical experience. We are not here deciding the question of whether "God" is experienced, or even presuming that such a question *could* be decided. The fact remains, however, that the mystical state cries out to be discussed on more than one level. To reduce it to an affair of simple psychology is to distort certain characteristics which belong to the mystical state, namely these two: (1) mysticism manifests an utterly transformed and non-ordinary consciousness, and (2) it is a state of being which completely bursts through the boundaries of my individual ego.

First, the meditative state is non-ordinary. Because it is so extraordinarily removed from everyday types of experience, there are no words to describe it. It is a state of non-thinking, rather than of thinking, of intuiting rather than of reasoning, of keeping quiet rather than speaking. In an effort to express this non-ordinary condition, mystics are driven to use dualistic language, to talk about a being or a level of being beyond the ordinary human dimension—and they speak of God, *Dharma, Tao, Brahman.* Are these mere psychological projections of an inner state of mind? Whether this question be answered "yes" or "no," the fact remains that the dualistic human-state vs. God-state language provides a more adequate model for describing the experience than does psychological monism. So dualistic language is demanded, then, by the very extraordinariness of the mystical state.

But there is another reason for the need to talk about the divine or transhuman, as well as the human. Mysticism is a state of being which completely bursts through the boundaries of my individual ego. When I cease to narrowly assert my little conscious self with all its filters, I become part of that which is greater than myself. Compare your ordinary everyday egotistic mind to a cancerous cell. It asserts itself and grows heedless of any relationship to the great body which supports it. What is the cure? Let this cancer remove its blinders, empty itself from its individualistic projects. Let it gently surrender to the life process and rhythm of the whole body. Such is the transformation realized in the mystical state. I live, now not I, but the Whole lives in me (or Christ does, or the *Tao*). I am a branch of the vine. I am a tide of the ocean. I am a channel of the divine life. I am an instance of the Way, and Everyman.

So it is no accident that the practice of mysticism is aptly expressed as an act of worship. In concentrative meditation I surrender myself to the power of the object, be it the flame, the lotus, the cross, or the mantra. I surrender myself to the source of being and energy which the object symbolizes. I let myself be filled by a reality beyond my skin, beyond my limited rational mind. Prayer is defined as a "raising of the mind and heart to God," a "standing in the presence of God." So meditation is an opening up of oneself to what is greater than oneself. It's an allowing of myself to live by the life of that mysterious Other of which I am a part. The rhythm and dynamic of meditation come close to that of worship. We do not claim that by meditation we can experience and "prove" the existence of a definite nameable "God." But I distort the mystical state when I flatten it out and reduce it to a mere matter of individual psychology.

I let go of ego to surrender to the Other: The duality of mystical experience. I experience myself as part of that other; I am it: the unity of mystical experience. In our self-assertive individualistic western world this surrender to the Other appears as a violent death of the ego. In the East, as we will see later in the book, it is a gentle letting go of an illusion. There is no such thing as a self that can live cut off from the Whole. The death of the ego is simply the death of an illusion, and nothing more.

We have dared to describe the mystic's reaching out for the very divine itself symbolized in images of centeredness, wholeness, and surrender. Does it seem to you too quick, too easy, too glib—this leap from ego to the Divine? If so, you are rightly skeptical. The cost is not cheap. The way of ascent to the divine is simple to talk about, all too simple. There is another path more modest, and more frightening because more realistic.

This other path is the path of descent into the self. Here, the objects of concentrative meditation do not symbolize the one goal, the Whole, or the Divine. Rather they are objects, images, and *mantras* designed to evoke this or that aspect or part of my unconscious self. The unity and wholeness of the meditative state are an illusion unless I am in touch with, accept, and possess myself fully. I must embrace my devils as well as my good spirits. I must know and accept my repressed fears, hatreds, blasphemies and libidinous energies as well as my conscious aspirations for the divine. Even the alchemists realized that one must have gold in order to make gold. In the path of descent, the way to wholeness is the long route through the teeming conflicting shadows of the unconscious self. It is small gain indeed if my two percent conscious self appears centered on the divine, and the ninety-eight percent rest of me is left behind in its accustomed murky confusion.

So there is *Bhakti-Yoga*, the path of devotion, for those who are not able, without danger of illusion, to proceed by the path of wisdom (*Prajna-Yoga*). And the Buddha speaks not only of *nirvana*, the goal of enlightenment, but of the demanding step by step Eightfold Noble Path. In later Buddhist Scriptures even this eightfold path is supplemented by instructions for meditation aimed not at *nirvana*, but, more modestly, at stages along the way. For example, the later Buddhists have listed as objects of meditation ten devices (e.g., earth, water, fire, air), ten repulsive things (e.g., swollen corpse, gnawed corpse, skeleton), ten recollections (e.g., morality, death, respiration), four stations of Brahma (e.g., friendliness, compassion), four formless states (e.g., station of unlimited consciousness, station of nothing whatsoever), and so forth.[3] Concentration on these images puts me in touch with various aspects of my human condition, with the realm of the body, the realm of death, the underworld of my self that my conscious mind might all too quickly by-pass.

The underworld of my psyche is not an easy place to be. Its images often partake of madness, hell, the satanic. So we come upon the devilishness of the Tantric tradition, the mad Greek god Dionysius, and Shiva, the Hindu god of creation and destruction. The fragile, precariously constructed world of my conscious self must be destroyed if the new self envisioned by the meditative state is to be created. The same neat world of my rational self must dare to confront and embrace its mad unconscious underpinnings if meditative Wholeness is not to be an illusion. I must consent to being possessed by the devil before I can be dissolved into that divine which embraces all, both devils and angels alike. It is perverse and idolatrous to make devil-worship a goal, but it may be a necessary stage in progress to the divine.

This descent into the self by meditation on those images which evoke the unconscious psyche, mad gods, and hell is at the same time a descent into the body. The lungs, the heart, the stomach, and the intestines provide a surer, if more circuitous, route to enlightenment than does the rational mind. The body need not be a dark curtain obscuring from the mind the secrets of the universe. Rather, the way of descent into the self sees the body as a microcosm mirroring and revealing the cosmos as a whole. By getting in tune with the secrets and rhythms of my own body I am by that very fact harmonizing myself with the secrets and rhythms of the universe. This respect for the body underlies both the practice of *Hatha Yoga* and the Ignatian "breathing" method of prayer, to cite examples from Orient and Occident.

The way of descent has the great advantage of de-romanticizing mysticism. The usual path of meditation does not lead to great visions, psychological "highs" and other-worldly insights. Such expectations are self-defeating. Expect nothing. See what results. Often it seems a dead end. Clarity dims. Enthusiasm dies. This could be progress unrecognized, as illusions are purged and readjustments take place to the reality of myself as it really is. As I sit in Sufi meditation concentrating on my rump, and sensing it and myself through it rooted to the earth, I am unlikely to be seduced by grandiose self-images or delusions of mystical prowess!

Yoga, founded by the Hindu philosopher Patanjali[4] (second century B.C.), is the system best known in the West for using the body to get control of the mind. There are eight steps to follow before one is capable of concentration, the final step in the practice of *Yoga*. The first step is *yama* or restraint, i.e., a life of self-control. Don't injure any living thing (*ahimsa*). Tell the truth. Don't steal or accept unnecessary gifts. Control carnal desires. The second step is *niyama* or culture. Cultivate good habits of eating, of cleanliness of body, of cheerfulness of mind, of contentment with one's lot, of enduring heat and cold, and of study of religious books. Only after one is cultivating such a way of life is he ready to practice the *āsanas*, i.e., the various yoga bodily postures.

The point of the *āsanas* is to make the body into a fit vehicle for concentrative meditation. The body must be free of disturbing influences if the mind is to be able to concentrate. The *āsanas* or postures are effective ways of keeping the body healthy and bringing the limbs and especially the nervous system under control so that they do not disturb the mind. The *āsanas* are not calesthenics!

Step four is *prānāyama*, the regulation of breathing. Aerobics in the West has stressed the relation between breathing and health of body and mind. Yoga goes further. Under expert guidance the Yogin learns to suspend breathing for long periods of time, thus enabling a state of mental concentration to continue undisturbed.

The fifth of these external aids to Yoga consists of withdrawing the senses from their objects, *pratyāhāra*. As long as the senses are captivated by their objects, inner stillness is impossible. Look at the faces of people passing you on the street. They walk in a trance, wrapped in a dream, drawn thoughtlessly in any direction by sense stimuli. The state of perfect control of the senses is very difficult to reach, but not impossible. And it is only after completing these five steps that I am capable of entering upon internal Yoga. Only after this external discipline am I able to start the practice of meditation properly so called! The way of descent into the body makes it clear that the road to enlightenment exacts a heavy toll. Apparent short-cuts are illusions.

Only after the demanding discipline of external Yoga am I ready for the final three steps of internal Yoga: attention (*dhāranā*), contemplation (*dhyāna*), and con-

centration (*samādhi*). Attention consists in keeping the
mind fixed on a single object, like the navel, the mid-
point of the forehead, the moon, or the name of God.
Contemplation consists of entering into the reality of
the object by long-continued meditation. And finally in
concentration, the mind is so totally absorbed in the object that it loses all awareness of itself. This is the state
of pure consciousness. Later we will describe how Yoga
philosophy understands this final state of liberation and
enlightenment. Our intent here is simply to cite an example of concentrative meditation which proceeds by
the way of descent. It is true, however, that in the final
stages of the Yoga method, the way of descent and the
way of ascent tend to merge and become one.

Let's sum up this discussion of concentrative meditation. Concentration is meditation by the use of symbols. By opening myself up to their action, I become
transformed by the Reality they symbolize. These meditation objects become instruments of "centering," of
self-surrender, and of harmony.

Further, these objects symbolize the paradoxes em-
bedded in reality. Their action enables one to live with
the dynamic tension between the polarity of life
through death symbolized by sacrifice, and with the
polarity of unity and duality which characterizes the
meditative state. The meditative state is not only a state
of psychological unity; it is a religious state which
bursts through the limits of individual psychology to a
level of being that transcends my individual self.

Next we discussed another form of concentration besides the way of ascent directly to this Other, this more-
than-myself. More circuitous and more secure, we saw,
was the way of descent into the self. A too precipitous
ascent and I'm in danger of leaving much of myself

behind. So I delve into the self through meditation objects which symbolize facets of my unconscious. My very body becomes a vehicle of descent into the self. We saw by way of example how Yoga uses this bodily path.

At their most profound reaches, the way of ascent and the way of descent tend to merge. The symbols become less important as the Reality symbolized takes over. Man is tempted to cling too tightly to the symbols. The symbols can cease to point beyond themselves. My mind can become like the Mexican art annex in New York City—a museum filled with faded tin ikons, mythic Huichol yarn "paintings," skeletons, demons, angels, devils, saints and papier-mâche dragons. This is the world of magic where symbol replaces reality and empty ritual replaces enlightenment. But the goal is meaning and reality, not symbol and reflection. While the outward path of concentrative meditation is guided by symbols, the two other types of meditation proceed without symbols. The negative way seeks knowledge of what the goal is *not;* progress is by elimination. And the inward-directed spontaneous path of *self-surrender* heeds the promptings of the meditator's own being toward his goal.

PICTURE OF GURU SRI BHAGWAN RAJNEESH LOOKS ON AS
DISCIPLE SURRENDERS SELF DURING "LETTING GO" MEDI-
TATION.   Photo by Ivan Spane.

III
The Negative Way

"You have heard how it used to be said, Do not commit adultery. But I tell you, anyone who even looks with lust at a woman has committed adultery with her already in his heart."[1] Harsh doctrine? Maybe. But real, inescapable, and true, so it had better be believed. My thought-life is absolutely crucial to who I am. Freud showed that for the unconscious, the thought equals the deed. The Far East taught this long before Freud and even Jesus. "All that we are is the result of what we have thought: it is founded on our thoughts, it is made up of our thoughts."[2] Control of mind brings control of self. I must dis-identify myself from false goals that the true goal may emerge. I must learn to enter the realm of silence. Only then will I come to know that there is a door opening within one somewhere. Only in stillness will I feel the key in the lock. The negative way of meditation is the process of recognizing false goals, wrong thoughts, enslaving desires. When I recognize them I begin to control them, and eventually eliminate them.

My thoughts and desires determine the destructive and distracting games I play. Until I know what I'm playing, I can't stop playing. Once upon a time, a Zen story goes, a monk was hiding a friend in his cellar. Two robbers came looking for this friend: "Tell us where he is." "I don't know," answered the monk. "If you don't tell us, we'll cut your throat," they told him.

"Since I am to die," the monk said, "I think I'll have a little wine." And he poured a glass of wine which he drank with complete equanimity. The robbers, flustered and consternated, went away. The monk refused to play the game of survival. In complete detachment, he chose to play connoisseur of wine. The robbers lost all power over him. My senses, thoughts, passions lose their power over me when I become aware of them, see through their game and refuse to play. With regard to our ordinary consciousness, we might take to heart the advice given by the madame to an apprentice prostitute: "Don't forget, you choose the men; not the other way around. And never say yes from exhaustion."

But you object that you know what you're doing. You're awake. You're aware of your goals, your thoughts and desires, and that they are under your control. I answer that mysticism provides a pathway to levels of consciousness undreamed of to most men. The great American psychologist and philosopher William James puts it this way:

Our normal waking consciousness, rational consciousness as we call it, is but one type of consciousness, whilst all about it, parted from it by the filmiest of screens, there be potential forms of consciousness entirely different. We may go through life without suspecting their existence, but apply the requisite stimulus, and at a touch they are there in all their completeness. . . . No account of the universe in its totality can be final which leaves these other forms of consciousness quite disregarded.[3]

The negative way of meditation works to eliminate "rational consciousness" so that the supra-rational might emerge. It detaches us from our normal working consciousness so that the unordinary consciousness might appear.

Ancient mystical tradition spells out three levels of "normal consciousness." If, by the negative path of meditation, we can detach ourselves from these, then the way is open to two "potential forms of consciousness entirely different." We'll describe in turn these traditional five levels of consciousness.

First, there is deep dreamless sleep. Consciousness ceases completely. Respiration becomes even. Heartbeat slows. Body temperature declines. In this state we must spend a large percentage of our lives as the price of bodily restoral. The state of dreamless sleep is a clue that self exists apart from consciousness and ego. As Jung points out, "However one may define self, it is always something other than the ego . . . surpassing it . . . not in the form of a broader or higher ego, but in the form of a non-ego."[4]

The second level of consciousness is dreaming sleep. This is quite distinct from dreamless sleep. Breathing becomes shallow. Blood pressure increases, as does the pulse rate. Rapid eye movements signal the occurrence of dream episodes. Like dreamless sleep, this dreaming state is essential to physical and mental health.

On the third level of consciousness, we are awake yet not self-aware, awake and not awake. Call it the state of "waking sleep." In Yoga philosophy it is called the state of "identification." Here we have our puppet man totally immersed, "identical with" every strong impression, every feeling, every stimulus that bombards him. He's the mechanical man. He *re*acts, he does not *act*. It is from this state of slavery to the higher realms of freedom that mysticism would lead us. I can change. It is my own floating unconscious choice to stay on the level of waking sleep. *Not* to choose otherwise is to choose to remain a slave. But there is an alternative. When I realize that this alternative is in my power, the whole quality of my life can change. And indeed it is in my power to move to the fourth level of consciousness —that of self-transcendence.

This transition is a leap from a flat two-dimensional life to a third-dimension. Everyone has glimpses of this new dimension at moments of "peak experience," perhaps under the influence of religious, sexual, or artistic emotion. I "remember myself." Not only am I aware of what I am sensing, feeling, thinking; I observe myself sensing, feeling, thinking. I am aware of what I do. And at the same time I have a sense of being separate from what I do. There is a sense of being detached from my physical body. As waking sleep is a state of identification, so self-transcendence need not be left to the chance occurrence of those "peak" moments of religious or artistic awareness. The negative way of meditation provides a disciplined path by which I might come to exist stably on this new level of being. Once I know it exists I have a hard and demanding choice to make. Do I continue to coast along in waking sleep, or do I undertake the arduous quest for freedom that comes from self-transcendence? The negative way of meditation will be the touchstone of the sincerity of my decision. Freedom does not come cheaply, and the negative way itemizes the cost. It's a decision about values. Will I choose to devote my life to the quest for higher levels of being rather than to the quest for higher levels of material possessions?

The quest for self-transcendence is not mad or esoteric. True, it involves mind-control, as we will see. But be careful. Under the rubric of mind-control today we hear talk about clairvoyance, clair-audition, telepathy, thought-reading, levitation, bi-location, and the like. Doubtless there is evidence for such phenomena. But self-transcendence is a much more stable, valuable and unromantic affair. Thomas Merton has said: "Prayer and love are really learned in the hour when prayer becomes impossible, and the heart turns to stone."[5] That is the hour that presents the challenge to the negative path of detachment, dis-identification, the entry into darkness.

There is a fifth level of consciousness, cosmic consciousness. It is a mindlessness, a no-knowledge. So far does it surpass the ordinary experience of being that Taoism calls it a return to non-being and ultimatelessness. Our map of the psyche is not like our map of the world where every square mile is surveyed, measured, located and described. The whole globe is familiar territory to us today. For men of an earlier age, the boundaries were unknown. The frontiers were populated by fantasy and imagination. All roads led to Rome in the center of the map. But move away from Rome, and the boundaries became shapeless and vague, and trail off into emptiness. So it is with the fifth level of consciousness. Even those who have been there have no words adequate to describe it. They invite you to leave the familiar territory in the center of the map and travel the increasingly arduous road to freedom in uncharted territory. Such is the negative way of meditation: a stripping away of the familiar to free oneself for the unknown.

We will concentrate on the shift from the third to the fourth level of consciousness, on the move from waking sleep to self-transcendence. Recall that my self-image, my thoughts, are crucially determinative of my behavior. Control of thought must precede control of behavior. The mysticism of the negative way is a path to thought control. I'll take a look at my thoughts, my self-image.

First I am located in space. I am at my desk on the fifth floor of an office building in Buffalo, New York, looking west over the main north-south traffic artery. If I could fly in the direction I look, I'd expect to arrive at California and, continuing, to come eventually to Hawaii, Tokyo, and the vast mysterious (to me) territory of China and Asian Russia. Because I visualize the world as a globe, I presume as I pursue my westward flight that I would pass over Europe, the Atlantic, and finally find my way back to Buffalo. My image of the earth as a globe is not as accurate as that of the international airlines navigator. I could not chart a "great circle" course from Europe to America. However I do know that if the downtown traffic on Main Street kept going south, it could reach Ecuador via the Pan-American Highway. And Canada, the Arctic, and eventually Russia again would greet the persistent northerly traveler. This globe hangs in space. I've seen it photographed from the moon. It is but a speck in Galaxy Milky-Way—which galaxy is but one of millions.

I am located in time. It's a week before election day and seven weeks till Christmas. I was born forty-four years ago. Receding gums, even sparser hair, stiffening joints, all signal that I am a terminal case. In three or four decades at the very most my time will be up. The dates 1492 and 1776 have meaning for me, as does 1066. Before that the birth of Christ, the exodus of the Hebrews from Egypt to the Promised Land, and the invasion of India by the Aryans occurred at thousand year intervals. Thence I look back into the increasingly dark reaches of unrecorded human life, preceded by the dinosaurs, the fishes, and the original amoebae. Clearly my space and time self-image differs considerably from the image that was current a little more than a century ago according to which the universe was created in 4004 B.C. and its center was the sun.

I am also located in the world of personal relations. There are houses to which I can go, and be sure of recognition and welcome as a guest. I am a professor. Students expect me to appear in certain classrooms at certain hours, lecture, give tests and grades. I have friends to whom I respond with affection and expect affection. I have a dentist who is not surprised when I walk into his office, recline, and open my mouth. But my bus driver expects me to keep my mouth closed and just put the token in the slot. In church, in the theater, and in the supermarket I play my appointed roles. And so I dance my way through various social games on the world stage.

I'm present in space and time, present in a field of social relations, but am I present to myself? Do I remain a mindless role-player moving through life toward death in a state of waking sleep? How can I cut the binds of habit, wake up, become present to myself, move to the fourth level of consciousness? The negative way of meditation precisely negates the limits of the third level so that the fourth may emerge. The eightfold discipline of Yoga and the practice of Zen meditation, *za-zen* ("just sitting"), are two methods of practicing the negative way. For now we'll take a less technical look at a method of stripping away consciousness three in order to open the door to consciousness four.

I presume you feel a call to move on. I presume you have intimations of a presence, a state of being, an unknown x, beyond the space-time-social world of waking sleep. In this sense, contemplation is a grace, a kind of transcendent gift. Your urge to respond signals that the invitation has been offered. Attention, awareness, and intentional activity are the antennae by which I tune in to this transcendent mysterious presence, a presence which is at once a call to unity (with the Self) and a call to otherness (a "divine" level of being).

Attention is the *sine qua non*, the first step to self-transcendence. In waking sleep, the attention is either enslaved, dispersed, or immersed. This is the state of identification. Non-identification involves attention which is *directed*. Enslaved attention is the crowd's mass hysteria at a Homecoming Day Notre Dame football game. By directed attention, on the other hand, I observe myself in attendance at the game and watch with bemused and affectionate detachment the crowd's mechanical responses to the vagaries of the pigskin moving up and down the field. Dispersed attention is wandering through the county fair, lulled by the scents of popcorn and cattle, the cries of barkers and children, the colors of holiday clothes and kewpie dolls. In a state of identification I float back and forth bathed in a sea of sensations. By directed attention, on the other hand, I observe myself walking and seeing and hearing. I am not lost in the crowd or lost to myself. Rather I watch myself as I walk through the crowd. I know exactly where I am and why. Immersed attention is the agonized checking and rechecking of bills, receipts and columns of figures in meeting the deadline for filing the income tax returns. In directed attention I am detached from the task even as I perform it. In a state of immersed identification I let myself become little more than a tax computer wriggling and grappling with obstinate figures. If I withdraw and create a psychic space between myself and my work, I live on a higher level. I compute, to be sure. But I am aware of being more than a computer. My attention ceases to be narrowly confined. It becomes flexible and open. I see myself as an object computing returns and hence not as self. In this way I transcend self and achieve a buoyant freedom as I act.

"What a man thinks, that he becomes." Identified with the football game, the county fair, the tax return, I become a mechanical reactor, without remainder. But when directed attention enables my thinking to transcend the mechanically reacting self, I become more than the mechanically reacting self. I become free. Even for the one-celled paramecium the "image," the "thinking," controls behavior. Heat the water in which the paramecium swims, and it swims rapidly in wider and wider circles looking for cooler water. In some primitive way it knows that water is divided into temperatures which are just right and those which are too hot for comfort, and it acts accordingly. Put a dye in the water and the paramecium will avoid it. But when it discovers the dye is harmless, it will ignore the dye. In some primitive way it has a memory of harmless dyes, and it acts accordingly. From paramecium to human being, thinking controls behavior and being. But man has that one great power not shared by the paramecium. Man can control thinking. How seldom man uses this great gift. He seems to prefer, like the paramecium seeking cooler waters, to swim round and round in mindless waking sleep.

This directed attention is a sentinel at the gateway of consciousness. Separate from the acting ego, the sentinel is aware of what the ego is doing, aware of the stimuli that call for its response. The sentinel can choose which impressions to admit, and which to reject. Degrading impressions no longer have free access to muddy, poison and pollute my mind. This discretion is not automatic. We need the sentinel. Otherwise there seems to be an almost perverse eagerness to allow the psyche to be polluted. We rightly dub television the "boob tube," but we don't turn off the set! The awareness of consciousness-four serves as both channel selector and off-on switch for the mind. From the state of waking sleep, I now become free and in control of my mind, and therefore of my being and behavior. I should be more fussy about what I let into my mind than I am about what I let into my stomach. Impressions which are freely and deliberately invited in bring with them an aura of freshness and wonder. And why shouldn't they? I am seeing them for the first time with awake and open eyes.

The negative way of meditation, then, is the ability to say "no." When I can say "no," there is born in me the wonderful new free power to say "yes." But how do I keep that sentinel awake in a culture which bombards me with sex, noise, advertisements, canned music, bells, and newsprint?

To leap to the practice of meditation without discipline of desire is useless, even dangerous. To say no to enslaving thoughts and desires means, of course, that I am not attached to the objects of those thoughts and desires. More than concentrative meditation the negative way highlights the decisive earnestness that must be brought to the quest for self-transcendence. It is not a task for dilettantes and faddists. It is no light undertaking to change the level of my being. Am I serious? Here are some questions I can ask myself to find out.

Am I willing to decide without reservation that my goal henceforth is to be spiritual enlightenment? To decide this is not to have accomplished it. But it is an essential preliminary. The materialistic siren songs of western culture will still sound in my ears. But a life-decision in the direction of a deeper happiness and a higher freedom will make them sound like honky-tonk. The decision is not a gloomy one. I renounce lower pleasures only because attracted by a higher joy.

Am I willing to take responsibility for my life without excuses or explanations? Whether I am crippled by a missing leg, an anxiety neurosis, or the scars of an unhappy childhood, that's me, period. I accept my past and take responsibility for it. I do not excuse present ir-responsibility because of past misfortune. There's no cosmic "fairness doctrine." If I am going to decide for spiritual enlightenment, I cannot fool around with excuses not to decide.

Do I accept my death? It is death that gives urgency to life. My time is short and uncertain. Like a hunter in the duck season crouched behind a blind, death is poised and has taken dead aim at me. The duck swims unaware, but its innocence of the hunter's presence does not make the hunter less present.

A short and uncertain life leaves time only for deci-sion-making. Time is too precious to be squandered in excuses, in explanations, or in attempts to please my friends or my culture. So I decide and, in deciding, ac-cept the consequences of my decision. My decision to go downtown shopping may result in my death under a truck or under a falling brick. So be it. In accepting the consequences of my decisions even unto death, I be-come free to decide and live. To point my life in the di-rection of spiritual enlightenment is to take a stand regarding my death, and hence regarding my life as well.

Am I willing to plan my activities, not rigidly but decisively? Will I act rather than react? Is my life a series of intentional choices or mechanical responses? Decision and intentional planning characterize the awareness of self-transcendence. I know what I am doing and why. When I find myself drifting into that mindless state of "identification," I stop. I begin again. What do I want to do and why? Fail to stop to ask this question, and planning sessions become personal wrangles, study sessions turn into daydreams, and at the supermarket dozens of brightly colored packages find their way into the cart beside the items on the shopping list. The drift from self-transcendence to waking sleep can be expensive for the pocketbook as well as for the spirit!

When, on the other hand, I act with attention, the work itself becomes its own reward. Aware that I am not the ego, I watch the ego play. Detached from the work, I act in freedom. The work is not me. I am not "identified" with it. I transcend it, and so move with ease and grace. No work is a matter of life or death. I live though the work fails because I was not the work to begin with. Detached from the results, I work better. Anxiety and fear of failure are not factors. Self-possessed and non-identified, there is no way the results can touch my core. Therefore I can delight as I watch my ego act its part in committee meetings, or match wits with supermarket "bargains" and packages, or unravel a book's secret in the study. Such are the joys of freedom for which I have traded mindless mechanical sense reactions.

Another question to test my seriousness: Am I willing to create for myself once a day, twice a day, an island of time when I will be still? I cannot expect all at once to start living in self-transcendence twenty-four hours a day, or even eight hours. But I can have daily "practice sessions." Stop. Be quiet. Sit still doing nothing. As the Zen saying has it:

Sitting quietly, doing nothing,
Spring comes, and the grass grows by itself.

So I practice self-awareness for one minute, five minutes, an hour—as long as I can. I observe my mechanical responses. I put my sentinel through his paces. By just observing them as they fly past like migrating birds, I learn what my thoughts and desires are. And gradually this awareness of what they are gives me the power to control them. I learn to say the "no" of the negative way. I learn what thoughts to encourage and admit, what desires to discourage and repel. I learn I have a sentinel and what his powers are. I learn my weakness too. The practice sessions faithfully performed will gradually carry over to the course of my ordinary life.

Am I willing to act against my main attachments? Here is the rub. Thoughts follow actions as much as actions follow thoughts. By self-transcendence, I become aware of the particular ways I am enslaved. But unless I act to rid my life of the enslaving objects, my awareness of enslavement is empty, transitory, and even dangerous. In the eightfold path of Yoga, the external disciplines precede the internal. If I am obsessed by cigarettes, homosexuality or gambling, step one to liberation is to stop smoking, to cut off homosexual relationships, to stop gambling. Detachment in thought is to be translated into detachment in life. The negative way cuts deeply. There is no escape from the double law of human life: first, I am what I do; and second, the source of hope: I do what I choose.

Action is the touchstone of the sincerity and depth of my commitment to self-transcendence. Action, too, reveals the strength and complexity of the bonds that enslave me. Repeated action builds the enslaving objects into my whole way of life. I tend to organize my life around them.

For the problem drinker, alcohol is not a liquid that one simply takes or leaves alone like orange juice or chocolate milk. Alcohol is a solution for psychological tensions; it's an essential ingredient of his social life; it's a ritual built into certain times of the day and days of the week; it affects the way he sleeps, and the way he makes love. Eliminate alcohol, and you shock not only his metabolism but his psychological balance, his social relationships, his daily routine, and his sex life. To top it off, you cause him insomnia! It's no wonder that the state of "identification" has such power to hold a man in the grip of waking sleep.

This focus on action, then, can be discouraging. But the bright side of the coin is this: External behavior can, after all, be changed. There's an alternative to smoking a cigarette: Throw the pack away. There's an alternative to watching TV: Turn the set off. There's an alternative to a dull job: Train for another, or lower your standard of living, or even go on welfare. Every action, however trivial or great, has an alternative. I can choose not to do it. And I can choose to do something else. This remains true whether I realize it or not.

There are two ways I can write my life's story. I can write it in terms of causality or in terms of freedom.

First, in terms of causality I can look for the reasons why I acted as I did. This will give me the explanation, the causes of what I am and have become. According to this picture, I was determined, programmed at each step along the way by the play of people, forces, and influences of my environment and temperament. It was inevitable that I turn out as I have. This is the explanation of me. My mother and father, my home surroundings, my religious and toilet training, my genetic structure punched out the IBM cards that dictated the blueprint of my character today. Such is my life story written in terms of causality.

That same story can be told another way—now from the viewpoint of freedom. Every action, every twist and turn in my life can be viewed not as inevitably caused, but as an alternative which I chose in preference to other alternatives which were possible but remained unchosen. Prove this to yourself. Make two columns. In the first write down twenty actions you performed during the past twenty-four hours. Then opposite each in the second column, jot down one or more alternatives that were open to you at that juncture (whether you thought about it at the time or not). Column one alone represents your life story in terms of causality. I did action "a" because . . .; I did "b" because . . .; then I did "c," "d," and "e" because . . ., etc. But read columns one and two together, and you can see your life in terms of freedom. I chose to do "a" instead of "a(1)" or "a(2)." I chose to do "b" instead of "b(1)" . . ., etc. I can view my life as a mechanical inevitable routine series of acts. Or I can see each moment as presenting alternative opportunities open to my free choosing.

The negative way of meditation supposes freedom

and awareness of freedom. Thought controls action. I
must be aware of an alternative before I choose it. And,
conversely, action controls thinking. For action tests
sincerity and roots the new way of thinking into the
sinews of my life. That's why it has been said: It is easi-
er to act oneself into a new way of thinking than to
think oneself into a new way of acting. Action without
insight is blind and deterministic. But insight without
action is impotent.

To sum up, in this chapter we have come the complete circle. At first, the negative way of meditation
focused on mind control for the sake of action. But the
dynamics of this quest led to the necessity of action
control for the sake of mind. We saw the five levels of
consciousness open to us. Outside of dreamless and
dreaming sleep, we ordinarily live at level three: waking
sleep. I have a rigid self-image of my place in space and
time and in the world of social relations. I therefore
play out my life on the world stage according to a
mechanically programmed script. The reason, paradoxically, is that in my self-image I am not present to
myself. I am not aware of, and therefore not detached
from, my acting ego and the objects with which it is involved. Negative meditation is a way of saying "no" to
this state of identification. We saw how self-transcendence comes about by the practice of directed attention.
Thereby I learn to say "no" to enslaving thoughts and
desires, so that I may say "yes" to higher consciousness, to responsibility for my own life, and to acceptance of my imminent death. Thereby I learn to say
"no" to automatic reactions so that I may say "yes" to
deliberate actions. I learn to say "no" to the whirlwind
of ordinary consciousness so that I may cut out for
myself islands of self-possessed higher consciousness.

Finally, I learn to say "no" to attachments and a causal view of life, so that I may say "yes" to alternatives in a life viewed as an exercise of freedom.

Surrender of attachment to and identification with what holds me down: This is the negative way of meditation. Meditation can involve, as well, not only a surrender *of* but also an attitude of surrender *to*. This is the third way of meditation, the way of surrender and self-expression which we will look at next.

HARE KRISHNA DISCIPLES (BHAKTI YOGA) CELEBRATING THEIR LOVE AND DEVOTION TO KRISHNA.

Photo by Ivan Spane.

IV
The Way of Surrender and Self-Expression

Apollo, the God of reason and discipline, guides the first two meditative paths of concentration and of negation. The third way of self-expression, however, is a surrender to the mad god Dionysius. Apollo says, "Here is a truth, contained in this symbol; concentrate on it and make it yours." Apollo says, "Here is a discipline, a system of detachment; practice it and make it yours." Dionysius, on the other hand, says, "Forget ready-made truths and traditional disciplines; abandon all structures; the truth lies within you; seek it within yourself—be faithful to your own unique voice." This is the path of surrender to the self and to the unpredictable and utterly unique forces that well up from the self. There are no pre-given objects. There are no formalized rules. The object is the self, and each self is unique. No pattern fits all. Each must find his own voice. Each must get in touch with the particular demons which possess him.

The Dionysian way is frightening in its very unpredictability and in the honesty it imposes. I can more readily deceive myself in the concentrative and even in the negative paths of meditation. I can imitate the ways of enlightenment. Objects of meditation are furnished me. I can concentrate on them with my rational mind and leave most of myself behind. I can deceive myself that I am united with the divine, when as a matter of fact I am united in thought alone and not in deed and in truth. I imitate and play at enlightenment. A path of discipline is laid out for me. I can abstain from the right foods and adopt the Yogic postures, while my attitude remains unchanged. I can imitate the outer trappings of detachment, while remaining attached to my own detachment. The objects and disciplines become ends in themselves, and obstacles to the very goal they were meant to assist.

The Dionysian way has no sacred mantras or dietary laws for me to misuse. *Chakras* and *āsanas* may predispose to enlightenment but they don't substitute for it. If misunderstood as short-cuts, they turn out to be dead ends. *Knowledge about* meditation and detachment is not meditation and detachment. No other man's power can bring *me* to the divine. If I am fortunate I will find a master and guide to help me find and nurture my own strength. But ultimately I am alone. Both the doing and the non-doing, both determined action and "just sitting" must come from my own center. As the Zen sutra puts it, "A poor man who counts another's treasure cannot have his own." That is why the meditative path of self-surrender points me right toward my own center. The truth is to be found within me.

No danger of too facilely assuming that what I discover there is divine. I will discover demons along with angels of light, hate as well as love, fear and despair as well as courage, attachment as well as withdrawal. Chuang Tzu says:

He who wants to have right without wrong,
Order without disorder,
Does not understand the principles
Of heaven and earth. . . .
Can a man cling only to heaven
And know nothing of earth?

They are correlative: to know one
Is to know the other.
To refuse one is to refuse both.[1]

In daring to embrace my own demons, I discover my own truth and divinity. The way to God may lie through possession by the devil, much like psychologist R. D. Laing finds the corridors of madness leading to sanity. Doubtlessly expressed in overly dramatic terms, such is the flavor of the teachings of Dionysius; such is the meditative path of surrender and self-expression. In less dramatic terms, respect and non-action are the keys to self-surrender. Let's look more deeply into these two characteristics.

This third type of spontaneous meditation shows the utmost respect for the self and for all the self's attachments. Enslaving impulses and sense objects are not spurned as *maya* or illusions but are treated with complete seriousness. After all, what could be more dangerous than the slave not taking his master seriously? My attachments are my manipulators. They keep me in line. They prevent my freedom. They punish me when I do not do their bidding.

Punishers are not less powerful when they are invisible. Teenagers will not engage in sex play in the presence of their parents, nor will muggers mug in the presence of the police. So they try to avoid their punishers. Police counter by sending out plainclothesmen and parents try to spy on their children. This in turn calls for methods of spy detection. But when the mugging fraternity is laced with informants, anyone might be a spy. The punishers are invisible and the control is complete. And when God takes over the job of spying on the teenagers, there is no escape from the eye in the sky. The punisher is invisible. The control is complete. So it is with my attachments in the state of waking sleep. Their invisibility makes their control complete.

So the meditative way of self-expression directs me to look within, and to treat with the utmost seriousness and respect whatever I find there, however hideous, bizarre, or "unspiritual" it might appear to be. Consider the yogi's advice to the young man who sat down quietly to meditate. Try as hard as he could, he was unable to keep his thoughts fixed on the eternal. His thoughts kept wandering to the image of his girl friend, her shape, her feel, their words and acts of love. The yogi showed him how to turn his weakness into strength. "Since you are so much attached to her," he said, "meditate upon her. See the beauty of her eyes, her hair, her skin. Feel the love that she has for you and you for her. Ask yourself what is the origin of this love. If she is the reflection, what must the source of such love and beauty be like?" The way of surrender respects my attachments. Only by confronting and coming to terms with them will I be able to transcend and free myself from them. The truth lies within me.

Like the successful ruler, I must give due respect to every citizen of the country. The ruler may well have the greatest wisdom and the best access to information. But he cannot afford to run the country in his own image alone. Old people and young people, farmers and urbanites, labor and management have their own image of the country, and act according to that image. Ignoring these other images does not make them go away. They remain present and acting. The more they are excluded, the more they will take their revenge either by open rebellion or subtle sabotage. My mind is like the ruler. Doubtless it is the wisest part of me. Perhaps for brief interludes I can manage to fix my mind upon the eternal. But I cannot afford to leave the rest of me behind. In this country of the self dwell other images, erotic, hate-filled, sensuous, demonic, terror-stricken, megalomaniac. Ignoring them does not make them go away. They remain present and acting. They will subtly or openly undermine any effort of the mind to act independently of them. The way of self-expression is the path by which I get in touch with the manifold, hidden, often conflicting parts of the self. The long-range goal is that not only the mind but the whole self in all its complexity will discover the divine unity in the process of self-unification. Respectful attention to the complexity of the process is the first characteristic of the way of self-expression.

Non-action is the second characteristic. Non-action, letting-be, succeeds where action fails. Action failed the young man with the distracting girl friend. Try as he might, he couldn't keep his mind off her. "Stop trying," was the yogi's advice to him. I don't have to try to be what I am. I am what I am without trying. To deceive myself about what I am, I do have to try. To pretend to be better or worse than I am, I do have to try. To make others think I am other than I am, I do have to try. By action, I try to fit the world and especially myself into my preconceived boxes. By non-action, I let go of my preconceptions. By not-trying, I stop the deceiving, the pretending and the image-making. When I let my being be, spontaneously of its own accord the I that was there all along finds self-expression. Such is the path of meditation by surrender to the self.

But non-action involves far more than letting go of my distorted and deceptive perceptions of myself. Non-action cuts far more deeply than that. It is by non-action that I bring others to respect my values and my way of being. Quite the reverse of Madison Avenue and Dale Carnegie! And more deeply still, it is by non-action that I break through the taken-for-granted world drilled into my head since infancy, and open out to the infinite and undreamed-of possibilities of this universe. We'll examine each of these in turn: non-action and other people, non-action and the taken-for-granted world.

Other people appear as the most formidable obstacles to my search for the truth that lies within and to the resolve to follow it. Dare to follow your own truth which is utterly unique and you risk being called non-conformist, crazy, selfish, peculiar, incomprehensible. How often I allow the opinions of others to write the script for my life. No wonder my own true image gets buried beneath the heap of conflicting and prejudiced images that others have of me. Non-action is the key to dealing with the host of uncomprehending significant others who would manipulate me—for my own good, of course.

Bodhidharma, the first patriarch of Chinese Zen, was asked by the emperor, "What is the first principle of Buddhism?" His wonderful reply: "There is no holiness." What did Bodhidharma mean? That saint and sinner, light and dark, yin and yang are correlatives? To affirm one without the other is to refuse both? Or did he mean that there is no ego to be called holy? That if the ego is an illusion, so too is holiness? Or did he mean that reality is value-free? It is neither good or bad. It just is. Whatever the meaning, the emperor did not understand it. What did Bodhidharma do? Launch into long explanations? No. He crossed the river and sat for nine years facing a wall in Shorinji. Non-action. Crazy, selfish, peculiar, incomprehensible? No matter what the emperor thought, Bodhidharma followed his own truth. In his own time the emperor might come to understand. Action would not hasten the day. Had Bodhidharma tried to explain himself, the burden of proof would have been his. Bodhidharma's non-action implicitly invited the emperor to seek the truth for himself. And, indeed, were the emperor to discover his own true voice, its words and accent would be quite different from Bodhidharma's.

Bodhidharma sat for nine years, it is said, until his legs withered away. Non-action need not be so dramatic. We choose to carry around on our backs the immense burden of the past. We choose, without realizing it, to live in a world tightly and restrictively defined for us from infancy. And so our actions are played out according to familiar patterns and long established routines. Non-action is a technique for shattering this taken-for-granted world. Maybe I am unable to envisage alternative ways of viewing the world, new possibilities of action, or undreamed-of ways of self-expression. If I can't yet make a new world, at least I can stop the old world. To stop the old familiar world—that is the secret power of non-action. I refuse any longer to cooperate in the process of maintaining that old taken-for-granted world image. Or at least by meditating for a certain period every day I stop playing the old familiar games and surrender myself to the unknown, to whatever may appear. This is meditation but without concentration on any special object. It is meditation but it does not seek for explanations. It does not ask "why," any more than the earth questions the wind. Rather, the earth gathers the seeds that the wind brings at any time the wind chooses to bring them. She nurtures the seeds, and they grow into grass and trees. Such is meditation by non-action. The seed of the self grows not mechanically but with the unpredictable rhythm and shape of something that is alive.

When I concentrate on particular objects, when I seek for explanations, I am in danger of going round and round in my treadmill ways of thinking. If you will be my disciple, hate your father and mother, Jesus said. My father and mother gave me that world that I now take for granted, that now seems so solid. Hate your father and mother—harsh words. No treadmill thinking here. But I'll break through to a new level of consciousness only if I bury the old. When a Hindu approaches his guru to devote himself completely to self-realization, the guru demands that he conduct his own funeral. The novice renounces all that had hitherto been himself. He buries his past, his name, his caste, his family. He renounces even his learning and his thoughts. In like manner Jesus says: Hate your father and mother.

My father and mother were the first to program me. They planted into my very heart and blood feelings of right and wrong, guilt and shame, duty and sin. My father and mother have a very definite image of me. There is a carefully constructed role and script that I am expected to play. There is no way in the world I can change that image or alter those expectations. As likely as not, when I am in their presence, I play my expected part. What is more, as likely as not, when I am not in their presence I play that expected part. If I am to be free of this burden, if I am to be either a disciple of Jesus or a Hindu *sannyasin,* I must hate my father and my mother.

Of course it is not only my father and mother I must

renounce. My friends, my enemies, and the people with whom I work, the TV I watch and the mail I receive all conspire to imprison me with their images. And so I obediently play the parts I am expected to play. I am sober and respectful in church, efficient and well organized in the classroom. I am properly elated when the home team wins and disapproving when my son brings home a bad report card. I obey television and buy toothpaste even though the dentist tells me that it makes no difference. I weep with those who mourn and laugh with those who make merry. My Christmas cards go out on time. I put my tie on for the expensive restaurant and take it off for Friday night's poker game. Such is the taken-for-granted world in which I live. My image of myself is given to me by others. My roles are defined and script-written. I play my parts to perfection. I am who others say that I am. But who am I really? Who do *I* say that I am? I really don't know. Meditation by surrender and self-expression is an effort to discover this real and hidden self. It is a way of non-action in order to break the grip of all these programmed actions.

So it was that Don Juan, the Yaqui Indian sorcerer, told his disciple Carlos Castaneda, "You have no personal history." My personal history is my life's story as told to me by my parents, friends, relations, enemies, and acquaintances, by my preacher, my psychiatrist, my lover, and my doctor. My personal history is the story of my needs and desires told to me by television ads and psychology books. Everyone in the whole world, it seems, is falling over one another in their eagerness to tell me my life's story, to tell me who I am. But who am I really? What story do I tell myself? I need not have a personal history, unless I choose to. I need not act out the pre-determined roles unless I choose to. I need not believe all my would-be biographers. My autobiography is mine to write if only I choose to do so.

How can I help mistaking for my real self these shadow images projected by others? What is more real than my bank's image of me, my employer's and my lover's? What could ever free me from their grip? The answer is easy. One day surely these shadow images will lose all hold over each one of us. That will be the day of our death. So I use my imagination. I conduct my own funeral now. My ghost hovers over my coffin at the wake. Where is my banker? What is my employer saying? What is my lover thinking? How real and important are the games I played at home, at work, at church? I don't expect it, but suppose that the wake were to be held the day after tomorrow—certainly possible. How would I spend my last full day on earth? How many of these mindless games would I play? What a pity to die without ever deciding for myself who I am and what I am living for.

The perspective of death, not death in general, but my death, shatters the complacent taken-for-granted natural world of waking sleep. Death is my great ally in teaching me how to live. Americans deny death, and hide their old people, thus losing the help of this ally. Death is nonetheless real for all that. It stalks me night and day. Any decision that I make could be the decision that will result in my death. To live responsibly is to accept the consequences of my decisions even unto death. It is to know that my life is my own to choose and that to dance to the images that others have of me is a grotesque squandering of my short and precious stay on earth. Meditation by way of surrender and self-expression seeks not the images of others, but the identity that wells up from my own depths.

Sociologist Durkeim tells us that "society is the walls of our imprisonment in history." Society is an objective fact. It gives me my beliefs. "You choose your beliefs by choosing your playmates," says sociologist Peter Berger. And, as we have seen, we are given our beliefs by "playmates" we never chose—parents, relatives, fellow citizens, fellow religionists. We have suggested meditation by way of self-expression as a way out of this pessimistic deterministic objective view of society. For as sociologist Weber has pointed out, society need not be viewed as an inevitably objective given fact of life. Social games are the creation of men. The world then is not a prison, but a stage on which we are the players. If it is a stage, I can refuse to be one of the actors. I can decide not to play the games. I can detach myself from my given roles. Meditative self-surrender is a way of detachment from socially given roles and scripts in order to discover and write my own.

Such detachment is easy to envisage but hard to practice. My indoctrination has been thorough. How do feelings, beliefs, and actions become so rigidly stereotyped? Sociology of knowledge outlines a five-step process by which society effectively makes itself into a prison for its members. Let's follow the birth of a simplified imaginary society. We start with a desert tropical island, of course. Have an Australian aborigine woman cast onto the south beach, and a day or so later imagine a former American eagle scout thrown onto the north shore. Uga and Bill—neither knows that the other is on the island. Uga gets hungry. She dives into the water, catches a fish, and squats on the beach to eat it raw. A few hours later, hungry again, she dives into the water, catches a fish, and squats on the beach to eat it. When hungry again she repeats the process. "Here I go again!" she mutters to herself. She is forming a habit. *Habitualization* is the first step we take in structuring our actions.

Things are much the same on the north shore. Bill, at his accustomed "mealtimes," gathers berries and nuts. In the best scout tradition he manages to build a fire. He roasts the nuts and eats. On getting hungry, he repeats the process. "Here I go again!" he mumbles to himself. Habitualization—his mealtime activity is settling into a fixed pattern.

After a few days, these lovely people spot each other. "I'm not alone," each thinks. Bill watches Uga, meal after meal, dive into the water, catch a fish, and eat. "There she goes again," he thinks. He casts her into a typical role. She's a fish catcher. This is *typification.* What was before a private habit has been transformed into a public type-casting. The public eye has further rigidified her habitual way of acting.

And when Uga sees Bill's mealtime ritual, she says to herself, "There he goes again." She casts him into a typical role. He is the fire builder, the berry eater. What started out as Bill's casual search for food has now been structured into a personal habit and a public role.

After a couple of days, Bill gets tired of nuts and berries. Fish would really taste good. He catches Uga's eye, and motions her over to the fire after she has caught the fish. He broils it. They both find it delicious. So, at the next mealtime, without any urging, Bill builds the fire and Uga brings the fish. A new mealtime routine is born. When they sit down to eat, they look at each other and say with their eyes, "Here we go again!" Their two separate roles, fish-catcher and fire-builder, have meshed. This is *institutionalization*. He expects her to catch the fish. She expects him to build the fire. Their mutual cooperation had made mealtime into an institution. What started as casual activity has become habitualized, typed, and now transformed into an institution. Their mealtime way of acting has become more rigidly solidified and structured.

Naturally enough, we imagine that eating together leads to sleeping together. And so in due course they produce a little son, Willie. Take a look at the world that welcomes Willie. The island for Willie is not an alien and once deserted spot. Rather, it is the whole earth. It's home. His father is everyman. His mother is everywoman. Consider how their behavior looks to Willie. He watches his mother and father at mealtime. He concludes that women catch fish. That's the way things are done. For Bill and Uga mealtime was a chance activity that eventually crystallized into an institution. For Willie, however, the way things are done at mealtime is an objective fact of life just as real as the trees, the beach, and the rocks. This is called *objectification*. Institutions harden into objective social facts.

Men build fires. Women catch fish. Willie can't imagine how things could be otherwise. But just to make sure he doesn't get any subversive ideas, just to make sure that "the stability of society is maintained," a final solidifying process enters in. This is called *legitimation*. A philosophy or a theology is born to "justify" why women *must* catch fish and men *must* build fires. Say, for example, that the first woman was sprung from the goddess of the sea, and the first man from the fire god of the mountains. Fish-catching is built into the nature of woman in the image of the primaeval sea goddess. And fire-building is the command issued to men by the father god of the mountains. So when Willie's descendents question why men and women behave as they do, here is a theology that tells the reason why. The social institutions of the island are *legitimated*. Men and women not only know how to behave. They feel that they *must* behave the way they do.

This rather lengthy excursus in the sociology of knowledge[2] is just one more way of spelling out the formidable task that confronts me when I try to discover the self that I really am. How many layers I have to peel away to arrive at the heart of my spontaneity: (1) action (2) overlaid with habit (3) overlayed with stereotype (4) frozen into institutions (5) that have become objective social facts (6) divinely and humanly legitimated. Meditation by way of surrender and self-expression is a way of subverting this taken-for-granted world. Looking into my own heart I question the legitimacy of the stories I've been told about myself. I come to see the subjective origins of these "objective" facts of life. Institutions lose their solidity and begin to appear as the games they truly are with their arbitrary rules.

Having pierced through the illusions which surround the self, what is this true self that I reach—*the* Self? God? No answer can be given to such questions. The very questions are destined to entrap the mind in the web of established, habitualized, institutionalized, objectified and legitimated thinking. The way of self-surrender is a surrender to the unknown—without preconceptions as to what might be revealed, and without desire for this or that revelation. I may find God or the devil, poetic voices or incestuous fantasies. I neither desire nor reject what I find. Whatever the revelations,

I accept and embrace them. For these are precious, invaluable signals from the unestablished, unpredictable, primal source of activity and energy. It is the illegitimate self, the self before it got born, typed, institutionalized, objectified, and legitimated. It's a fullness I never get to see while in the mechanical state of waking sleep.

Clarke's Law asserts, "When a distinguished but elderly scientist states that something is possible, he is almost certainly right; when he states that something is impossible, he is very probably wrong." I tend to judge possibility and impossibility by the yardstick of my natural established thinking patterns. And so even in something so intimate and personal as self-identity and self-knowledge, I allow myself to be defined by others. What *they* say is impossible, I accept as impossible. And so I never come to know the range of my own possibilities. That's a tragedy which meditation by way of self-surrender is designed to avert. I simply have to get in touch with signals that come not from society but from the undreamed-of possibilities of my own self.

Society has my thinking about myself organized. What doesn't fit is "impossible." It has been said that "incompetence is directly proportional to the degree of organization." Organization puts things in pigeonholes, and people in cages. To change the metaphor, I operate on only two of my eight cylinders. In fact, I don't even know that I was meant to have eight cylinders. Hence my incompetence. I sputter my way through life in fits and starts less than one-quarter alive because less than one-quarter conscious.

Can a short meditation period each day change all this? What difference can five or ten minutes, a half hour, or even an hour a day make? A lot. When I tune in to the radically new signals issuing from myself, they will eventually subvert my established thinking patterns. The whole of my consciousness is more than the sum of its parts. When you change a part, you change the whole. When a married couple have their first baby, there's much more at stake than just "one more mouth to feed." The whole household is disrupted. When husband and wife become mother and father, the quality of their relationship to each other changes. There is a shift in their entertainment habits, their sleeping patterns, their schedules of working and of love-making. To surrender daily by meditation to the signals from my own self is to bring a new baby into the house of my consciousness. I will never be the same. My safe, established, secure, mechanical prison world is subverted. My relationships to others begin to shift. My roles don't appear so inevitable. Ethical imperatives take on the character of stage directions or rules of the game. The signals received during meditation disrupt my life during the rest of the day. With this new baby in the house of consciousness, even my entertainment habits, sleeping patterns, schedules of working and love-making come under question. I find myself unable to blindly take them for granted anymore.

In a word, daily meditation changes the ecology of the mind. The first rule of ecological responsibility is to realize that the biosphere is a whole which is greater than any of its parts. Consequently, if you change the part, you necessarily change the whole. When I spray a beach with DDT to kill the flies, I discover, as did the U.S. Navy, that not only do I kill the flies, but I kill the fish as well. And the dead fish washed ashore invite ten times the number of flies that were there originally. "Change the part, you change the whole." This ecological law teaches one thing. Never underestimate the power of a relatively small interference to have an impact on the whole system. From a fly's eye point of view, the killing by DDT of flies in a small area turned out to be a gastronomical boon to the survivors of the species. In the realm of mental ecology, ten to sixty minutes a day of surrender to the self is small enough interference in my regular conscious patterns. But change the part, and you change the whole. There will be repercussions on the whole conscious system.

To sum up this chapter, the meditative path of self-surrender is taken under the tutelage of the mad god Dionysius, mad because he reveals the darkness as well as the light that resides in my depths. Eschewing an overly quick leap to divine union, I pay respectful attention to the complexity within myself. My attachments are taken seriously. Only by working them through will I come to a self-unity which is not an illusion. My competing, often contradictory passions and drives must be taken into account before I reach my unitary goal.

This surrender to the self is just that, a surrender, a letting go. Non-action is the key. I let go of trying to be good. Rather than masquerading as a good man, I face and accept both the evil and the good in myself. I let go of my concern for other people's images of me. More profoundly still, the way of non-action loosens the grip on me of the ordinary taken-for-granted world. To the extent that this happens, my self opens out into unsuspected possibilities. This letting go of my culture's established definitions of the world is the import of Jesus' harsh command to hate your father and your mother. I must recognize and see through the images of myself that exist only in the minds of others. In this process of letting go, death is my ally. Like it or not, death will break all the constricting bonds of the taken-for-granted world and of the images and expectations of others. So why not make that break now, and live a life with the freedom that comes with death?

But the imprisoning walls of the taken-for-granted world are thick indeed. A fivefold process petrifies the rock which makes these walls. From birth my patterns of thinking and acting are privately structured by habit, publicly stereotyped by others, and then locked into institutions, which institutions take on an objective reality of their own and receive the stamp of philosophical and theological legitimation. My culture is one of many perfectly arbitrary ways of structuring the world. The fivefold process of habitualization, typification, institutionalization, objectification and legitimation makes it appear to be the inevitable and only way.

That is why the meditation of self-surrender does not look to this world for its signals. It rather tunes in to the unpredictable spontaneous signals issuing from the self, the illegitimate self. A new baby introduced into a household subverts the established routines and causes a restructuring of the whole family's life patterns. Even so, just a little daily meditation subverts my established taken-for-granted world. I begin to see its arbitrary character and, in seeing it, become free from it, free to listen to and follow my own unique voices.

These first four chapters have dealt with mysticism as an experimental psychological reality. The interpretation of that reality has deliberately been left vague and ambiguous. An experience, of course, is susceptible of many and differing interpretations. Just what is this "self" we have been talking about? Is it different from the body? Is *my* self distinct from yours? Is there just one Self, or are there many selves? Is God involved in mystical experience? If yes, is it a theistic God or pantheistic? What is the precise path to self-realization? In what does self-realization or liberation consist? The Hindu, Taoist, and Buddhist traditions give their own answers to these questions. In the following chapters we will review the varying interpretations of mystical experience offered to us by the Orient. We turn first to India and the most ancient of all traditions, Hinduism.

SHIVA-RAM—INDIAN DANCER DEMONSTRATES OPENING OF
THE THIRD EYE, PSYCHIC CENTER WHICH IS DEVELOPED
THROUGH THE PRACTISE OF YOGA. BEHIND IS THE SAN-
SKRIT SYMBOL FOR OM—PEACE.

Photo by Ivan Spane.

V
Hinduism

Christianity has a long and great mystical tradition whose spokesmen include John the Evangelist and John of the Cross, St. Augustine and St. Bernard of Clairvaux, Meister Eckhardt and St. Teresa of Avila. There is no need to disparage it. But it is especially fitting that we look to Hinduism for our first interpretations of mystical experience, and this for four reasons. The first reason is *age:* India, together with China, has the oldest continuous cultural tradition in the world. The *Vedas*, which are the Hindu sacred scriptures, began to take shape around 2000 B.C. with the Aryan invasion of India. They are revered and followed as the revealed source of Truth even to the present day for hundreds of millions of people. Second, Hindu mysticism is *practical.* It focuses squarely on the rules of *how to live my life.* All the theories, stories, and rituals have this one goal: to lead me to self-liberation. No philosophy is worth doing if it doesn't have a practical repercussion in my life. Third, Hindu mysticism is thoroughly metaphysical; it gives an all-embracing, comprehensive, cosmic account of mystical experience. Transcending the partial explanations of psychology, sociology, or biochemistry, it shows how my individual mystical experience plugs into the universal order of things. Finally, the Hindu interpretation of mystical experience is absolute. In its highest form it's not tied down to this or

71

that culture. It claims to be based on Absolute Reality itself, and Absolute Reality knows no cultural or national boundaries.

There are six classical systems of Indian philosophy.[1] In other words, there are six basic ways of interpreting the *Vedas*. Of these, the two best known in the West are *Vedanta* philosophy and *Yoga* philosophy. We will therefore concentrate on these two systems. They might better be called *viewpoints* rather than systems. In the West, philosophical systems tend to be competitive and antagonistic: British Analysts won't talk to French Existentialists. But the Indian is very much at home with differing viewpoints. He would readily see *Vedanta* and *Yoga* as merely alternative paths to the same goal of liberation.

Vedanta and *Yoga* are both orthodox philosophies. The touchstone of orthodoxy in Hinduism is not belief in God. No, it is rather acceptance of the authority of the *Vedas*. Neither Buddhism nor original *Yoga* philosophy accepts the existence of God or of a divine reality. But *Yoga* is orthodox. Buddhism is not. Buddhism rejects the authority of *Vedas*, whereas *Yoga* philosophy reverences the *Vedas* as a source of sacred and infallible truth. All orthodox schools agree in accepting the *Vedas* as revealed truth.

Secondly, all orthodox Hindus accept the doctrine of rebirth from life to life. The idea that one human life span is generally sufficient for self-liberation is preposterous to the ordinary Hindu. And since there is rebirth, there also is a soul or a self that gets reborn. In the West we can find it worthwhile to discuss whether there is a soul and whether it is immortal. The immortality of the soul is a problem for us. For the Hindu, the existence of the self and its continual rebirth until ultimate liberation is a fact of life. It's something "everybody knows." There's nothing to discuss. It simply isn't a problem. No one would dream of questioning a doctrine which seems so self-evident and clear. As we will see, "self" and "liberation" receive varying interpretations, but the "rebirth" framework is always assumed.

The doctrine of rebirth is a consequence of the law of *Karma*. Indians both orthodox and unorthodox have a firm faith in an eternal moral order in the universe. No action is without its effects, and its effects are never lost. "As you sow, you shall reap." The law of *Karma* is a law of conservation of moral values, of merits and demerits of actions. There is never any escape from the consequences of what I do. And whatever happens to me is itself a consequence of my own past actions either in this incarnation or in a previous one. There are virtuous men who are miserable. They are suffering the *Karma* from a previous life. We see wicked men who seem to be happy. They will not escape the *Karma* that flows from their evil deeds. All actions motivated by passions and desires are governed by this law. Only selfless detached activity does not produce these binding fettering consequences. Actions performed without self-interest not only entail no enslaving effects, but they help destroy the accumulated effects of my past actions done under passion and self-interest. Through such deeds done with detachment the self gradually escapes from bondage and rises above the law of *Karma*. When totally free, the self finally escapes from the wheel of birth and rebirth.

The law of *Karma* does not encourage a kind of despairing resigned fatalism. And non-attachment to the consequences of action does *not* mean indifference. *Karma* is a law of realism and hope, not of indifference and despair. It is realism. Actions do have consequences. And I am responsible for these consequences. For example, Mahatma Gandhi took full responsibility for the violence which his civil disobedience campaign unleashed. Sincerity and good intentions alone are not enough. Whether I remember it or not, consciously or unconsciously, I have made myself what I am. And however I might try to avoid it, I remain responsible for the effects of the actions I do now. This realism is a source of hope. There is a way of escape from bondage, the path of non-attachment. Actions done perfectly for their own sake without passionate and anxious concern about the results are actions which lead to freedom. The fatalistic indifferent man performs his actions in a slovenly way. He feels no responsibility for his own life. The law of *Karma*, however, is an invitation to the responsibility and freedom that comes with detachment. Whether *Karma* is interpreted as an impersonal law or as the dispensation of a personal God, the Indian has no doubt that there is a moral order which pervades the universe. This is a fact accepted by all, and needs no discussion or proof.

In addition to the authority of the *Vedas* and the law of *Karma*, all orthodox Hindus accept the existence of an ultimate Reality, call it heaven, call it a personal Lord, or call it the impersonal divine Absolute *Brahman*. Not all Hindus believe in a personal Creator God who rules the universe, the image of God so familiar to the West. This denial of a personal Creator God I can call atheism. But such atheism is not irreligious. It is perfectly compatible with the doctrine of salvation or release from the cycle of birth and rebirth. This denial of a Personal Universal Ruler is compatible with prayer and sacrifice offered to lesser deities existing *within* the realm of my experienced world. And finally, this "atheism" can express a thrust toward a level of Absolute Being. This thrust would be a leap beyond a God who is pictured in the all too human images of "ruler," "creator" and "person." So however *atheistic* some forms of Hinduism may appear, *irreligious* they are not. Quite the opposite. Hindu philosophy is at its heart and essence profoundly religious. And this is especially true of the system of *Vedanta*.

Vedanta represents *par excellence* the philosophical viewpoint of modern Hinduism. *Vedanta* is the face of Hinduism that contemporary India shows to the West. Among Hindu intellectuals *Vedanta* is the most vigorous and influential system of Indian philosophy. Shankara (born about 788 A.D.) is the founder and guiding light of this way of interpreting the *Vedas*. His major commentary on the *Vedas* is the *Brahma-Sutra*. The metaphysical point of view is uncompromising *monism*. In other words, in the last analysis reality is basically One, basically Divine. Differences, distinctions, and changes are therefore to be considered illusions. Hence Shankara's metaphysics is called *Advaita Vedanta*, i.e., *Non-Dualistic Vedanta*.

As in all the India systems, right away we are caught up in the consideration of the nature of reality itself. This is no idle speculative consideration. My view of reality cuts right to the heart of my view of myself, and I had better have the right story if I am to find the best path to liberation. *Yoga* tells a *dualistic (dvaita)* story about Reality and therefore about myself. *Vedanta* tells a *non-dualistic (a-dvaita)* story about reality and therefore about myself.

Vedanta demands from me one great act of faith. If I accept this one truth, everything else follows from it. What I am to believe is this: *The Self is God*, i.e., *Atman* is *Brahman*. Why should I believe it? Because it is the teaching of the infallible revealed *Vedas*, those very same *Vedas* that have been the guide for hundreds of millions of people for almost four millennia. The burden of proof lies not with one who would defend the *Vedas*, but with the man who would reject such a long standing, successful, and widely accepted authority. *Brahman* (God) is *Atman* (the Self). The goal of life is to realize existentially this central Vedic doctrine.

Brahman is not a personal God. Better call *Brahman* Absolute Reality. The Absolute is the fundamental reality of all things. Everything is a manifestation of *Brahman;* everything *is Brahman*. This is not merely a teaching to be accepted on Vedic authority. The goal of mystical experience is to experience and realize this for myself, namely, that *Brahman* is Absolute Being, the Reality of all realities. *Brahman* is *sat* (Being).

Brahman is also *cit* (consciousness). Not only can I discover *Brahman* in the world by the outward path of concentrative meditation, but also the path inward to my own conscious self leads to *Brahman*. The realization of *Brahman* as *cit*, as pure consciousness, is the goal of the negative way of meditation. *Atman* is experienced as *Brahman*.

Brahman is also *ananda* (bliss). Happiness is this experiential realization of *Brahman* as Being and Consciousness. The meditative path of self-surrender is at its most perfect point an experience of pure Bliss. *Sat cit ananda*—Being, Consciousness, Bliss—these are the three aspects of transcendent *Brahman, sat chit ananda* —these are the three dimensions that describe the state of self-liberation (*moksha*). *Sat chit ananda* is the goal where the meditative paths of concentration, negation and surrender all merge into one.

This is beautiful mystical language. The trouble is that it is just that—language. Words cannot capture the experience that lies at the profound first level of truth. The realization that *Brahman* is *Atman* is the goal of all mysticism, of all life. To accept this truth on authority is one thing. To realize it experientially is something else. While I might have passing glimpses of this profound level of truth, my everyday common-sense life is lived at quite another and more superficial level. *Vedanta* philosophy realizes this, and proposes a theory of double truth or two-level truth to explain the contradiction I feel between the Vedic teaching about *Brahman* and my everyday experience of life.

The problem is this. If there is only one Reality, *Brahman*, then what do I make of my common-sense experience that reality is not one, but many. I seem to experience the existence of many selves, many animals, many trees, many changes, many feelings, many births and many deaths. Clearly if *Brahman* is all there is, then this common-sense experience of plurality is an illusion. And indeed such is the Vedantic teaching.

I can understand this "metaphysical illusion" by comparing it with the more familiar illusions that happen in my everyday world. Suppose, for example, I see a rope (this is a true and real perception), and I mistake it for a snake (my interpretation is an illusion). I really do see a rope: the illusion comes from my wrong in-

terpretation. So it is with *Brahman* on the one hand
and my everyday experience on the other. I really do
see *Brahman*. My illusion comes from not realizing this
and interpreting my experience as if there were really
many selves and many beings and as if these many individuals were not merely manifestations of *Brahman*,
the one and only reality. It's not that the experience of
my senses is false. I really do sense what I sense. What
is wrong is that I don't have the right viewpoint, the
mystical insight that would help me see the everyday
world for what it really is. And so my experience is an
illusion. It's not exactly false. It's wrong-headed. The
world of illusion has its own kind of truth. It's a second-level truth. First-level truth would be to experience this world and myself from the standpoint of its
and my own identity with *Brahman*. Such is the Vedantic analogy of illusion:

$$\frac{\text{rope (true perception)}}{\text{snake (wrong interpretation)}} = \frac{\text{The One Brahman}}{\text{appearance of many individuals}} = \frac{\text{First-Level Truth}}{\text{Second Level Truth}} = \frac{\text{Reality}}{\text{Illusion}}$$

The man of wisdom lives in this world of multiplicity, change, and appearances just as everyone else does.
But he is not fooled by appearances. He knows from
the authority of the *Vedas* that the appearances are just

that—appearances. The manifold beings that strike his senses on all sides are manifestations of *Brahman*, the one Divine Reality that pervades all things. More than that, the wise man through the practice of mysticism actually experiences and sees this world through the eyes of *Brahman*. His self (*Atman*) is *Brahman*. It is not an individual ego that knows this world. Rather *Brahman* is the Knower, and *Brahman* is the known. There is nothing that is not *Brahman*.

The ignorant man, however, takes appearances at their face value. All the multiplicity and change is taken to be real in itself. He thinks his individual mind and ego is a real being in a world of many other selves and beings. Like the wise man, he lives in the world of appearances. But to the ignorant man, these are not appearances, but are reality itself. He has no higher point of view. He does not see the divine masquerading in sensible form. So he lives in illusion, mistaking the appearance for the reality.

God masquerading, God the Magician, God the great illusionist—these images based on the *Vedas* are part and parcel of the Vedantic way of explaining the cosmos in which we live. Just as there are two levels of truth, so there are two levels of explanation of what the world is all about. The first level, as we have seen, focuses on God as transcendent and on mystical insight. There is no *maya* or illusion. The myriad forms of the universe are experientially realized to be manifestations of but one divine reality, *Brahman*. The cosmos reveals *Brahman* to the wise man. The second level, however, focuses on the cosmos as concealing the immanent God. Creation is *Lila*, "God at play." Like a Great Magician, God conjures, and we take the appearance for the reality. So it is with those who live at the second level of truth.

Creation, then, is God at play. It is, as Alan Watts puts it, God pretending not to be himself.[2] The game is hide and seek. And so we individuals don't know who we are. We are God, of course, but God who has forgotten his divine identity. The few enlightened ones, of course, see through *Lila*, the cosmic game. The others, however, heedless of who they are, take the games for real. To these ignorant ones then, these games are not games at all. And life is not *Lila*, the divine dance, but deadly earnest involving work and suffering and pain. Part of the joy of mystical insight is to see the world through the eyes of the Magician, where the grim world of human work and suffering dissolves into a vision of divine play.

"Why did God make the world?" I once asked an Irish friend of mine. "For laughs," was his answer. His spirit was nearer to the Hindus than to the Hebrews. In the book of Job, suffering, death and tragedy are transcended. They remain real, but are viewed as parts of an inscrutable whole. The *Gita* tells a different story, of tragedy not transcended but denied. The heart of the *Gita*, the most revered of Indian Scriptures, is a dialogue between the devout Warrior Arjuna and Krishna, an avatar or incarnation of the god Vishnu. Duty commands Arjuna to take part in a great civil war. Arjuna balks. He has no stomach for slaughtering his kinsfolk. What greater tragedy is there than civil war that turns brother against brother and father against son. But Krishna explains that it is illusion to take the war at its face value. What appears to the ignorant man as "tragedy" doesn't even belong to the world of the real.

Krishna tells Arjuna: "Thy tears are for those beyond tears; and are thy words words of wisdom? The wise grieve not for those who live; and they grieve not for those who die—for life and death shall pass away. . . . From the world of the senses comes . . . pleasure and pain. . . . They are transient. Rise above them, strong soul. The man whom these cannot move, whose soul is one, is worthy of life in Eternity. The unreal never is; the Real never is not."[3]

Tragedy and pain exist only for those who mistake the world of illusion for the Real. I suffer only insofar as I am bound to this world of *maya* or illusion. "*Yoga*," the *Gita* tells us, "is the breaking of contact with pain." In a previous chapter we outlined the steps by which *Yoga* mystical discipline gradually detaches the self from the world of suffering and illusion. *Vedanta*, along with the other Indian systems, uses the techniques of *Yoga* for its mystical quest. *Yoga* is an ancient practical path to mystical experience. The *interpretation* of the experience will vary according to the philosophy of the mystic. For example, Christians, Buddhists, and Hindus all have mystical experience. But they differ from one another in the interpretation of their experience. *Atman* is *Brahman* is the *Vedantic* interpretation. Enlightenment is interpreted to be a realization of *monism*, namely, that the self and all things are God. Not surprisingly, *Yoga* borrowed by *Vedanta* is interpreted in *Vedantic* terms.

The philosophical world of original *Yoga*, however, is not monistic but *dualistic*. The *Sankhya* system ("Distinctionism") is the metaphysical backdrop for original *Yoga*. In the *Sankhya* world, spirit and matter are distinct. Unlike *Vedantic* monism which says that everything is basically spiritual and divine, *Sankhya* philosophy sees the world made up of not one but two kinds of stuff, Spirit and Matter, or better, Selves (*purusha*) and Nature (*prakriti*). The relationship between *purusha* and *prakriti* is the key to understanding Yogic mysticism. Here's why.

In the Hindu view of creation, the universe had no beginning. Like the individual, the universe itself goes through successive cycles of birth, growth, and death or dissolution. The story of a creative cycle is the story of how Spirit gets involved with Matter. The evolution of the universe comes about from the progressive *union* of *purusha* with *prakriti*. It is important to understand this, because Yogic mysticism is an effort to reverse the process. *Yoga* is a *devolution*, a process of *separating purusha* from *prakriti*. We will consider first the make-up of Nature, Matter, or *prakriti*. Then we will outline how it evolves when it is joined by Self, Spirit, or *Purusha*. Finally, we will enumerate the stages of Yogic mysticism which reverses the process and brings about the separation of *purusha* from *prakriti*.[4]

Prakriti is the ultimate, unconscious, active, basic "stuff" from which mind, body, and all things are made. If there is only this one basic kind of stuff, where does all the variety in the world come from? *Prakriti* is composed of three forces (*gunas*), and this explains the variety. All things are made up of various proportions of (1) buoyancy (*sattva*), (2) energy (*rajas*), and (3) mass (*tamas*). Or in emotional terms call them: pleasure, pain, and indifference; or another translation, brightness, force, and inertia. Before creation begins, *sattva* (pleasurable buoyant brightness), *rajas* (the painful power of energetic force), and *tamas* (the heavy mass of indifferent inertia) are in a state of equilibrium. No one of these three dimensions of *prakriti* prevails over the other.

But when (due to contact with the Spirit or Self as we will see later) creation begins, the various realities of this world take their different shapes and qualities. The three *gunas* begin to combine in varying proportions, and the particular "recipes" according to which *sattva, rajas,* and *tamas* are blended will determine the particular qualities of created things. When one of these three forces predominates, it tends to subjugate the others. An abundance of one of the *gunas* in a being will cause the being to resemble that one. *Tamas* predominates in a slab of marble because of its inert mass and resistance to activity. Fire with its searing energy has an excess of *rajas.* The human mind abounds in *sattva,* the force of brightness and light.

The *gunas* are also mutually supportive. They depend on each other for their operation. Each conditions the other two and is in turn conditioned by them. An idea (*sattva*) alone is impotent unless there is energy (*raja*) to carry it out and a field of resistance (*tamas*) into which to introduce the idea. Energy alone is chaos unless it has intelligence to direct it and resistance to contain it. A fallow field (*tamas*) of itself lies unproductive without a plough (*rajas*) to furrow it guided by the shrewd (*sattva*) farmer's hand.

So *prakriti* is the basic cause or stuff out of which everything is made. Nothing comes from nothing. Therefore there must exist a basic material principle (called *prakriti*) from which all things come. But the beings of this world are remarkable for their variety and differences from each other. Therefore, *prakriti* must be composed of different forces to explain this great variety. So we conclude that *prakriti* is composed of three forces, *sattva, rajas,* and *tamas,* whose permutations and commutations result in the complex and variegated world of our experience. Before creation, these three forces are in a state of equilibrium. How does it evolve into the world as we know it?

Prakriti alone is unconscious, non-intelligent, blind. *Purusha* alone is a passive principle, inactive. Evolution demands that the activity of *prakriti* be guided by the intelligence of *purusha. Purusha* is like a lame man carried on the shoulders of the blind man *prakriti.* The cooperation of Spirit and Matter, *purusha* and *prakriti,* brings about the world that we know. Recall how the story of creation begins in the first book of the Hebrew-Christian Bible. It tells of the Spirit hovering over the primaeval chaotic waters. So the Hindu process of creation starts when *purusha* contacts and disturbs the primaeval equilibrium of *prakriti. Rajas,* the most active of the *gunas,* is first disturbed. And through the movement of *rajas,* the other two *gunas* begin to vibrate. And in the tremendous commotion that ensues, the *gunas* join in various proportions and combinations to form the objects of the cosmos.

Creation, then, is a process in which pure consciousness, or *purusha,* gets progressively more and more bound up in the world of Nature, or *prakriti.* Creation is an evolution outward, from Spirit to Matter, from pure simple consciousness (*purusha* alone) to complex enslaved consciousness (*purusha* involved with *prakriti*). The first product of creation is Mind (*chitta*). The mind seems to be intelligent, but it is not. It's *prakriti.* Like a mirror it reflects the intelligence and consciousness of *purusha*. The mind records impressions gathered by the external senses (*manas* = the recorder), classifies them (*buddhi* = the classifier), and attributes them to a particular individual ego (*ahamkar* = the ego-sense). This is the first step in *purusha's* fall from purity. *Purusha* sees its reflection in the mirror of the mind and mistakes the reflection for the original. And the mind starts to claim intelligence for itself, and the ego starts to say "I" am the knower. *Purusha* itself, the true knower, remains unknown. The mind, a mere instrument of knowing, usurps the role, like an electric light bulb claiming to be electricity.

The first product, then, of *purusha's* contact with *prakriti* is mind. Evolution continues with the production of the five senses (sight, smell, feeling, taste, touch), the five organs of action (tongue, feet, hands, and evacuative and procreative organs), and the five sensible qualities (sound, feel, aspect, flavor, odor). These last combine in various proportions to produce earth, water, air, fire, and ether—the elements of which the cosmos is composed. So pure consciousness gets progressively more involved with matter. Each added layer is grosser than the one before, as *purusha* is successively bound up with mind, the senses, the external body, the sensible qualities of things and finally with the five gross elements which make up the external world.

Each added layer of matter involves *purusha* more and more in ignorance. Forgetful of its identity as pure consciousness, *purusha* mistakes itself to be an individual mind living in a sensible body involved in a world of material things. The essential self in me, the true knower, remains unknown. I attribute intelligence to my mind. I live on the surface concerned about my body, buffeted by my sense experiences and worried about material things. I mistakenly think that if I am robbed of my possessions, my "Self" is robbed, that in experiencing sickness and pain, my "Self" is at stake. But, as we see from the story of creation, *purusha* or Self is not mind, or ego, or body, or senses, or material things. It is a case of ignorance and mistaken identity. Mind, ego, body, sense, and things all evolved from *prakriti*, with the cooperation of the separate and distinct principle of pure consciousness, *purusha*. If I would realize my true identity, I must realize my identity with *purusha*, and not misplace my identity in the world of mind, body, and matter which holds me in its bonds.

This analysis takes us beyond the average American drugstore paperback view of *Yoga* as a type of calisthenics. *Yoga* is evolution in reverse. Evolution is the story of *purusha's* progressive involvement with *prakriti*. *Yoga* is the recipe for *purusha's* progressive detachment from *prakriti*. In Chapter II, *Yoga* was cited as an example of concentrative meditation by way of descent into the self. There we outlined the eight practical rules or steps laid down by Patanjali in the path toward enlightenment. Here we will point out the seven stages in which this enlightenment or perfect knowledge of *purusha* is reached.

The first stage is the realization that enlightenment lies within one's own heart. I can travel the world over from shrine to shrine, go from master to master seeking counsel, and read Scripture upon Scripture, but in the end I must realize that the Self I am looking for is the reality of my own life. Since the source of all wisdom lies within me, there is no obstacle to attaining it except my self.

The second stage of enlightenment is the cessation of pain. As I begin to focus on the Self, I see that it is distinct from the fears and aversions of the body and the mind. I am not my body. I am not my mind. Physical and mental hopes and fears cannot touch the self when I realize that *purusha's* reality is distinct from the world of *prakriti* where body and mind exist. In this way the *Gita* says: "*Yoga* is the breaking of contact with pain."

The third stage is one of complete union with the Self. "Like a hailstone melting into the ocean," as Shankara says, do I blend into and merge with *purusha*. The objective universe of experience disappears. I see and hear nothing. This is *samadhi*. I know only the joy of the eternal self distinct from time and change.

The fourth stage is my return from the ecstatic state of *samadhi*. I am conscious again of the eternal world, but no longer am I deceived by my apparent identity with that world. I live and move in it, but I know reality for reality and appearance for appearance, and give each its due. I walk the earth like everyone else but view it with an awareness springing from my true Self. My actions are truly voluntary with no mixture of compulsion from past *karma*. Ordinary moral rules don't apply. The saint is a man beyond good and evil.

The fifth stage is the realization that the time has come to leave this world behind. The mind, the body, and the cosmos, by the process of Yogic meditation which is evolution in reverse, have served the purposes of the Self. The Self uses the world to be free of the world. *Prakriti* is the ladder climbed by the Self. On reaching the top, *purusha* kicks the ladder away.

The sixth stage is the death of the saint, a death that breaks the wheel of birth and re-birth. The ideas and memories stored up in the mind fall away. The mind as an instrument has done its job. The *gunas*, too, fall away. Liberated *purusha* needs the services of *prakriti* no longer.

The final stage is that of eterna! existence as the Self. The Self realizes that it has always been distinct and pure and alone. It will know that the mental and bodily world of *prakriti* followed its own laws. These laws were never the business of the Self. It was through ignorance that the Self was involved with them and, as it were, lived in a foreign land. It was an alien in that land because it was an alien to its own true identity. This is the final state, *purusha*, self-sufficient, peaceful, calm, painless, blessed, never again to be deluded.

Such is *Yoga* philosophy's way of interpreting the mystic's experience of enlightenment. Our brief look at the *Vedanta* and the *Yoga* philosophies gives us some idea of the unity and the complexity of Hindu mysticism. Both are orthodox, i.e., they look to the *Vedas* as the authoritative source of their basic doctrines. Both philosophies are, above all, practical. They preach a way of liberation from the cycle of birth and rebirth. Both accept the doctrine of *karma*, that my present condition is a consequence of my past actions either in this life or in previous lives. Neither can I escape the consequences of my present or future actions. "As you sow, so you shall reap." Actions performed under the influence of passion keep me bound to the body and the world, and so cause me to be reborn again and again.

Both *Vedanta* and *Yoga* agree that it is ignorance of my true reality, my true identity, that keeps me chained to the wheel of birth and rebirth. For both *Vedanta* and *Yoga*, this ignorance consists in thinking that my ego, my body, my senses and the material world are part of who I really am. *Vedanta* and *Yoga* both teach that liberation comes through knowledge and insight into who I really am. Finally, for both *Vedanta* and *Yoga*, the way of mystical insight is one path to this enlightenment. All these points of agreement define the typically Hindu way of viewing the world and the human predicament.

But, as we have seen, Hinduism is not a monolith. The Hindu experience, similar in so many respects, receives radically differing interpretations from *Vedanta* and from *Yoga*. These two orthodox systems differ especially in their views of (1) the nature of the material universe, (2) the nature of the Self, and (3) the existence of a divine Reality, *Brahman*.

Nature taken at face value is *unreal* for the *Vedantist*. It is mere deceptive appearances, second-level truth at best, whereas nature for the Yogin is one of the two ultimate real principles of the universe. It is *prakriti*, the basic stuff out of which all non-personal things are made, and the locus of all evolution and change. Mystical enlightenment for the Yogin consists in this realization, namely, that nature is what it is; nature is the non-personal material principle of all things and is not to be confused with *purusha*, the personal conscious principle, whereas the Vedantic mystic's enlightenment consists in realizing the unreality of nature, namely, that what appears to be nature isn't really nature at all, but *Brahman* in disguise.

The two schools differ in their interpretation of the self. The Vedantist sees the Self or *Atman* as the one and only reality of all things personal and impersonal. And this one basic reality is divine. Mystical enlightenment, then, consists in precisely this realization, namely that *Atman* and *Brahman*, and, appearances to the contrary, the apparent reality of sensible things, are *maya* or illusion. *Yoga* philosophy, on the other hand, is dualistic. The self is one of two real principles which together, *purusha* and *prakriti*, cause everything that is. Here, then, mystical enlightenment consists in realizing precisely this, namely, that *purusha* is indeed a distinct and real principle and not part of that changing world of Nature where dwell the ego, the body, the mind, and the senses.

Finally, *Vedanta* and *Yoga* differ in their views about God. Whereas for the Vedantin everything is divine *Brahman*, the *Yoga* system, at least in its pristine form, is atheistic. The Vedantin sees his enlightenment as the realization of his own divinity. At his deepest level of reality, he is divine. *Atman* is *Brahman*. The Yogin, however, views his enlightenment as the realization of his own self. He is *purusha*, pure consciousness. This mystical insight breaks him out of the cycle of birth and rebirth into changing world of *prakriti*. Later forms of *Yoga* introduced the notion of a supreme Lord. Like Ishvara in *Vedanta* philosophy, this Lord furnished an object of devotion and path to enlightenment for ordinary folk for whom the way of mysticism was too exalted and austere. Basically, though, in *Vedanta* and *Yoga* we have two orthodox systems of Hinduism, one pantheistic, the other atheistic. Despite the profound differences in their interpretation of the world, the self and God, they both live in the unmistakable Hindu world of the *Vedas*, of *Karma*, and of self-liberation through release from ignorance by mystical insight. The orthodox Hindu of whatever persuasion is friendly and at home with both.

We move now to a heresy, an unorthodox system. Let's enter the thought world of Buddhism.

TANKA—REPRESENTING YAMA, THE LORD OF DEATH, ONE OF THE MANY MYTHOLOGICAL DEITIES FOUND IN TIEBETIAN BUDDHISM, AS WELL AS THE ANCIENT HINDU SCRIPTURES— THE VEDAS.

Photo by Ivan Spane.

VI
Buddhism

Siddhartha Gautama died about 487 B.C., revered as the "Buddha," which means the "Enlightened One."[1] The hard historical facts about his life are even scarcer than the verifiable accounts available concerning Jesus, the "Christ" (the "Anointed One"). These minimal facts are reasonably sure: The Buddha was the son of the chief of the Shakya tribe; he gained enlightenment under a sacred pipal tree at Gaya, in modern Bihar; he spent many years teaching and organizing his followers; and he died at about the age of eighty. But whereas Christianity developed into a religion centered on its founder Jesus Christ, the Buddha warned his followers against focusing on him. As we will see, each man was to follow his own path and listen to the promptings of his own heart.

Though the historical facts are few, as with Jesus the Christ, the traditions surrounding the life of the Buddha are rich, and have inspired his devotees down through the centuries. His father is believed to have been a king, an orthodox Hindu of the highest Brahmin caste. Prince Gautama grew up in a religious household but was at the same time surrounded with luxury and sen-

sual pleasure. His father made every effort to shield his
son from all contact with suffering, poverty, and the
evil side of life. The king even forbade him to venture
forth outside the palace grounds. When the time came
to arrange a trip for the prince into the city, the king
ordered that all the aged, the crippled, the maimed, and
the sick be kept off the road. But the gods wanted to
open up the prince's eyes to the human condition. So
they created an old man with gray hair, hobbling along
with a cane, his eyes dim and sunk deep in his face, his
limbs weak and bent. And the prince asked, "What
happened to this man? Was it an accident, or is this his
natural state?" And so the prince learned about old
age, the destroyer of beauty and strength. He learned
that this man had once been a baby and then a hand-
some youth. But now that man was ruined by old age,
his memory gone, deprived of pleasure, his sense organs
dulled. And the prince, deeply moved, asked, "Will this
happen to me too?" And having been assured that the
ravages of time are indeed inescapable, Prince Gautama shook his head despondently and asked to return
home. "How can I enjoy the palace gardens anymore,"
he thought to himself, "when the fear of old age and
death prey upon my mind?"

And indeed the palace seemed empty to him, and the
prince grew more and more restless. Again he asked to
go into the town, and again the king agreed, having
given orders that all signs of suffering be kept away
from the prince's path. But the gods, still intent upon
opening Gautama's eyes to the human condition, created a man whose body was ravaged by disease. "What is
wrong with this man?" asked the prince. "His body
quivers when he breathes; his belly is swollen, his legs

limp, his shoulders and arms emaciated, he whimpers in pain." The prince learned that this is the great evil called disease, that this man had once been strong and healthy, but disease had laid him low, and that disease was not peculiar to this man but the common lot of all.

And in like manner on a third visit to the city, Prince Gautama saw a corpse. "What happened to this man?" he asked. "Carried by four others, he is well-dressed, but the people who follow him are in tears." The prince was told that this man was without mind, breath, senses, or power, that he lay unconscious like a log of wood, that the people who followed behind had cherished and cared for him with affection but that now he was a corpse to be abandoned and burned like a bundle of dead grass. And the prince also learned that this state was not peculiar to this man, but that death was the final state of all men however high or low their dignity on this earth.

Gautama was despondent. He marveled at how people could heedlessly seek pleasure and enjoyment when they knew that old age, disease, and death were the certain and inevitable lot of all. His social status, his religious traditions, his family's ambitions for him became ashes in his mouth. He left home to undertake the lonely individual quest for salvation. The luxuries of palace life had failed him, so he took up for six years the course of harsh asceticism. That failed him, too. So Siddhartha Gautama sat under a pipal tree (also called the "*bodhi* tree," "the Tree of Wisdom") to meditate. He vowed he would not rise from that position until he had attained his goal. And after seven days and seven nights he was enlightened. Siddhartha Gautama became the Buddha. The content of that enlightenment formed the core of Buddhist doctrine to be outlined in the rest of this chapter.

We will see that Buddhism involves a switch in focus (1) away from the *Vedas* to personal responsibility, (2) away from a substantial self and God to the insubstantiality of the flux of experience, (3) resulting in a fresh diagnosis of the human predicament, with (4) the consequent injunctions regarding salvation.

The *Vedas*, as we have seen, are the touchstone of Hindu orthodoxy. Buddhism's rejection of the authority of the *Vedas* immediately puts it in the camp of the unorthodox systems as far as Hinduism is concerned. Where is the authoritative source of truth, then, for the Buddhist? Responsibility for discovering and following the truth is planted squarely on the individual's own conscience. This is epitomized by the Buddha's final injunction to his disciples: "Work out your salvation with diligence." No scripture, no revelation, no teaching (not even from the Buddha himself) can tell me my own truth. My own path is one which I must discover alone and walk alone.

Of course I can receive the advice of others, listen to the teachings of the Buddha, and even read the Scriptures. But these ideas that come to me from the outside must be put to the test. And the test is that of my own experience. I cannot rightly evade the responsibility of asking myself, "Does this work for me in my own life? Do I see its truth for myself?" One might almost say that the Buddha anticipated American pragmatism by some two and a half millennia! The test of truth is in the consequences that it has for my own living. The focus is squarely on experience.

This pragmatic experiential attitude is one reason

why many disaffected Christians who look to the
Orient for enlightenment find a haven in Buddhism
rather than in Hinduism. For in the latter, they would
simply be trading the authority of the Church or the
Bible for that of the *Vedas*. Buddhism, however, places
religious autonomy completely in the hands of the individual seeker. In rejecting the tyrannies of legislated
morality, he is challenged to find the way for himself.

Buddhism is pragmatic in another way, too. It is
short on speculation, and long on practice. Whenever a
disciple would ask idle, theoretical, speculative questions, the Buddha would bring him right out of the
realm of theory back to the present, to the now, to experience. Life is like a house that is on fire. Things are
not as they should be. There is pain and there is suffering. The need for salvation is now. While your house is
burning down, you don't idly sit back and speculate
about what might have been the origin of the fire. This
is not time for speculation. You take action. You find
water to put the fire out.

But it's not just the urgency for action that led the
Buddha to put the damper on cosmic speculations.
Some questions have answers (e.g., "Is it raining out?"
Answer: "Yes, so wear your rubbers"). Some questions
are answerable, but I don't have the information (e.g.,
"What's the deepest crater on the moon?" Answer: "I
don't know"). Finally, and this is what concerns us,
some questions are unanswerable. In fact, they
shouldn't even be asked, because when you ask them
you are in danger of thinking that there is an answer
somewhere if you just look hard enough. Such is the
question put by the disciple, "What is the origin of the
heavens and the earth?" to which the Master replies,

"What is the origin of your question?" First of all, such a question, even if it were answerable, has no bearing on your practical life here and now. More importantly, such a question is wrong-headed. It shouldn't even be asked. "What is the origin of your question?" In other words, what makes you think that there *is* an origin to the heavens and the earth? Even to answer such a question by saying "I don't know" or "No one knows" puts the Master in a false position. It would dignify the question by assuming that there is an answer somewhere, but no one knows what it is. Such questions do not deserve to be so dignified. They spring from the human need to construct systems of thought by assigning causes and reasons to things. But reality remains mysterious. It resists all our efforts to box it in by our human constructs, systems, and rationality. The proper response to mystery is not speech. The proper response to mystery is silence.

So the characteristic Buddhist approach to reality is through the silent non-rational path of mysticism. What rationality cannot grasp can be touched by concrete mystical experience. Buddhism does not attempt to say what reality *is*, but rather is content to state what it *is not*. Reality is not *Atman*. Reality is not *Brahman*. There is no substantial self. There is no substantial God.

In place of a doctrine on *Atman*, the self, Buddhism teaches *anatman*, the doctrine of "no-self." If you want to picture the nature of the self and reality, think of a river. Or think of the "stream of consciousness," to use the image of William James (the founder of pragmatism). What I call the self is really a stream of thoughts, sensations, feelings, desires, and ideas. I am like a river, never still, but with ever-flowing processes, digestive processes, eliminative processes, emotional processes, conscious processes, ever-changing state following upon state, no one instant like the previous instant or the instant that is to come. I talk about "the self" as if there were some unchanging core, some underlying identity, some substantial reality beneath and behind this flowing stream of processes. In other words, I ask one of those unanswerable questions, "Who is it who is thinking, feeling, digesting, and sensing?" And then I answer the question, "It is the self, the soul, *Atman* who thinks, feels, and senses." By asking a question that never should have been asked, I get trapped into an answer that never should have been given. What does experience show me? Not a self, a soul, an *Atman*, but simply a stream of thoughts, feelings, sensations. By the test of experience I see that there is thinking, there is feeling, there is sensing. I don't experience a self that senses, a soul that feels, an *Atman* that thinks. The rational mind does not respect the mystery of this flowing conscious stream. It wants to freeze it, define it, put it in an identifiable box. So it asks the unaskable question, "Who is it who thinks?" Where does such a question come from? Who said there should be anybody or anything who thinks? The question comes from the grasping, domineering, rational mind that does not respect mystery. But experience shows that the question is a wrong-headed one. Surely, if you invent a wrong-headed question, you already imply a wrong-headed answer. It's like the famous question of the divorce lawyer, "Have you stopped beating your wife?" The jury is trapped into assuming that the defendant has at some time beaten his wife. So when I ask "Who is it who thinks?" I am trapped into assuming that there is a somebody who thinks, a substantial self or *Atman*. In Buddhism such a problem is not solved, but dissolved. Rather than give an answer, the Buddhist does away with the question. Experience shows me streams of processes, not a "self." This is the basic Buddhist doctrine of no-self, *anatman*. We will see its immense significance. The illusion of having a "self" is our great source of pain and suffering. Salvation for the Buddhist consists in "letting go" (*nirvana*) of this illusion.

But first, an objection: What about the personal pronoun "I"? What about an individual's own name, e.g., Richard M. Nixon? Don't these refer to a permanent individual self? The Buddhist teacher Nagasena answers by the famous comparison with a chariot. What indeed is a chariot? It is not the axle, not the wheels, not the spokes, not the frame, not the reins or the yoke. Nor is a chariot something other than all these separate parts. There is no chariot soul or chariot essence. "Chariot" is simply a practical name or label I give to the particular combination of components which make up this vehicle. Richard M. Nixon is simply a conventional tag or label given to that flux of biological, sensitive, and conscious processes that flows in and around Washington, Key Biscayne, and San Clemente. The name Richard M. Nixon should not fool me into postulating an unchanging permanent individual R. M. N. *Atman* lying underneath all the processes. Nor should the personal pronoun "I" delude me into trying to freeze my streaming river into a block of individual ice to be defended. protected, and clung to at all costs. This delusion of individual identity is the source of all anxiety and pain. Peace comes by realizing that the pronoun "I" is simply a label like "Mississippi"; then letting go of egotistical fantasies, I am free to flow with my ever-changing stream.

So in Buddhism there is reincarnation, but no transmigration. There is no soul or self to migrate from one life to another. But the stream does go on. It takes up in another life where it left off in this one. Nagasena uses the metaphor of a flame. Suppose I have a lighted candle, and I pass the light to another candle, and from there to another and another. There is no individual flame migrating from candle to candle. So it is with myself. One state of consciousness follows upon another, one incarnation follows upon another, instant by instant as flame follows upon flame. Such is reincarnation without transmigration.

Just as there is no underlying self or *Atman*, so too there is no basic essential Reality or *Brahman*. Don't call this nihilism or even atheism. It is out of reverence that the Buddhist refuses to define or capture the self. The mysterious flowing stream defies all rational efforts to pin down an essence and an identity. I can be mystically in tune with the human flow, but the mystery of the person escapes all rational understanding. Buddhism tells me what it *is not*. Only mystical intuition can put me in touch with what it *is*. The same reverence and silence in the face of mystery characterizes Buddhism's approach to cosmic reality. The name God or *Brahman* does not come easily to the lips. Indeed such a name is not pronounced at all. In rejecting the doctrine of *Brahman*, Buddhism shows that the mystery of Reality escapes all rational understanding. Our human constructions, definitions, philosophies, and names of

God are seen for what they are, human constructions. *Nirvana* is "letting go" of these human efforts to grasp, freeze, and contain Reality. In the state of *nirvana*, what exactly does one see? To answer such a question would be to return to the world of human rationality which *nirvana* has transcended. Thus Buddhism heeds the philosopher Wittgenstein's injunction, "Of that whereof one cannot speak, one must be silent."

Clearly, then, cosmological and metaphysical speculations do not characterize the teaching of the Buddha. No, his doctrine is eminently practical, psychological, and concrete. After his enlightenment under the Tree of Wisdom, Gautama Buddha proceeded to the Holy City of Banaras, where he found five ascetics, former companions, in a deer park outside the city. To them he preached his first sermon thereby, as the tradition says, "setting in motion the Wheel of the Law." The chariot wheel in India signifies empire. The Buddha was setting out to establish an empire of righteousness, much as Jesus preached the Kingdom of heaven. Gautama called his path the "Middle Way." He had learned in his youth at the palace that the pursuit of pleasure does not bring happiness. He learned during his years as an ascetic that the other extreme of harsh self-mortification is equally futile. The "Fourfold Noble Truth" contains the essential teaching of the Middle Way between these two extremes.

The Fourfold Noble Truth is like a doctor's diagnosis and prescription. The Buddha has a cure for what ails mankind. The first noble truth diagnoses the disease (*dukkha*, the universal fact of sorrow). The second tells the cause (*trishna*, different cravings as the cause of sorrow). The third truth gives the cure (*nirvana*, the stopping of all cravings as the stopping of sorrow). The fourth noble truth prescribes the medicine (the Eight-fold Noble Path leading out of sorrow to enlightenment, *satori*). We'll look at each in turn.

Recall the shock of young Gautama when he first left the haven of his palace gardens to encounter old age, disease, and death. These are the inevitable lot of mankind, and yet mankind flees from them, denies them, incessantly struggles against them in a battle that is doomed to failure. Anxiety, then, and sorrow are the diseases that infect mankind. Every contact with the unpleasant causes this sorrow and anxiety. Every separation from pleasure is sorrow (*dukkha*). Every unfulfilled wish is sorrow. This is the First Noble Truth of Sorrow or Anxiety (*dukkha*), the universal disease of mankind. Age, sickness, death, suffering—these are not the disease. No, these are universal facts of the human condition. Anxiety (*dukkha*) about age, sickness, death and suffering—this is the disease. This is the universal flaw in the human condition that the Buddha sets out to cure.

To cure the disease, one must know the cause of the disease. This brings us to the Second Noble Truth which concerns the origin of Sorrow or Anxiety. A Buddhist parable from the Zen tradition illustrates it well. Once upon a time, the story goes, a man was being hotly chased by a tiger. The tiger was gaining on him, when the man realized to his horror that he had run to the edge of a cliff. Quickly he grabbed onto a bush growing at the edge and swung himself over the side. There he was hanging on the side of the cliff, the tiger roaring down at him from above. He looked down. Another tiger was roaring at him from the foot of the cliff. As he hung there in midair between them, he noticed a little white mouse and a little black mouse nibbling away at the roots of the bush from which he was hanging.

We'll finish the story in a minute. The man, of course, is everyman, each one of us. Here I am hanging midway between birth and death. I can't go back to the cliff top, back to the womb from which I came. And certain death waits for me at the foot of the cliff. What anxiety—that universal human disease of *dukkha*—as I notice that time (the two little mice) is nibbling away at the roots of my survival! I must surely die. I don't want to die. Yet I'm helpless to prevent it—whence anxiety and sorrow. I'd like to be young again, to go back to the top of the cliff. But that can never be. I am powerless to reverse the march of time—whence anxiety and sorrow.

The cause of my sorrow is *trishna*, craving, clinging to desires that can never come true. I tell myself I shouldn't be hanging there on the side of the cliff. And yet, inevitably, there I am. So I torture myself with anxiety. I want the peaceful life I used to have at the top of the cliff. And so I pine away with regret. I fear my future fate at the cliff bottom as time goes on and my grip gets weaker and weaker. So I struggle against the inevitable with increasing frustration and anguish. I regret the past. I fear the future. I rebel against the present. Craving to be other than I am, clinging to the desire to be who I am not and where I am not—this is *trishna*, the origin of mankind's universal sorrow. This is the Second Noble Truth of Buddhism.

Now back to the side of the cliff and the Third Noble Truth, the cure. Everyman is still there, but now no longer looking up to the top of the cliff and the mice nibbling away, his gaze no longer fixed on the tigers roaring at him from above and from below. He notices juicy strawberries growing on the bush to which he clings. He plucks one in his lips. How good it tastes!

And this is the end of the story—*nirvana.* The cure for craving is to let go of craving. The way to be who I am is to stop clinging to the desire to be who I am not. *Nirvana* means "letting go." I let go of desire instead of vainly trying to satisfy it. The past is past. I accept it without regret. It no longer need preoccupy my attention. I surrender myself to the flow of time, thereby relieving myself of the impossible need to freeze it or reverse it. I accept the fact that the process of my living naturally flows into death. Fear of the future no longer transfixes me. I am free to see the strawberry, this present moment which is all that I have. How good it tastes! This is Buddhism's Third Noble Truth.

Note that *nirvana* is expressed in negative terms. It is a process of stopping the craving, letting go of desire. What is *nirvana* in positive terms? What does the saint in the state of *nirvana* positively see? This cannot be put into words. *Nirvana* is a transrational mystical state. It is a release from the human cravings. To attempt to express *nirvana* positively in words would be precisely to return to the human categories which the state of *nirvana* leaves behind. Buddhism is not a prophetic religion based on the preaching of the word. It is a mystical religion with mysticism's mistrust of words.

The most illusory category of all is that of individual ego. As long as the man on the cliff believed he had an individual ego at odds with its environment, an individual ego to be preserved against the ravages of time and the fate of death, he lived in sorrow brought on by these impossible cravings. But when he let go of ego, and surrendered himself to the flow of time and the flow of life enjoying each present moment and each successive conscious state, then, freed from impossible cravings, he lives in the state of *nirvana*. He has attained enlightenment (*satori*). Enlightened while on this earth he is the saint (*arhat* or "worthy one") living in empirical *nirvana*. Released at death from the wheel of rebirth, he is at peace in the state of transcendent *nirvana*.

Lest this enlightenment sound selfish and cold, note, too, the ideal of compassion that developed in the Buddhist tradition—the *bodhisattva* ideal. The *bodhisattva* is the Buddha-to-be. He is enlightened, but he postpones the peace of *nirvana* in order to show others the path, just as Gautama Buddha got up from under the *bodhi* tree to bring his Fourfold Noble Truth to others. He brought them not a speculative doctrine but a program for action, a prescription for their ills. The first Three Noble Truths give the disease, the cause, and the cure. The Forth Noble Truth is the doctor's prescription, the Eightfold Noble Path to Enlightenment, a manual for the practice of the Middle Way. The first two steps call for Commitment: (1) Right Understanding, (2) Right Attitude of Mind. The next three propose an Ethics: (3) Right Speech, (4) Right Action, (5) Right Livelihood. The last three cover the mystical dimensions: (6) Right Effort, (7) Right Awareness, (8) Right Concentration.

When I intellectually grasp the Buddha's teaching and my motives are not selfish but compassionate, then I have the proper commitment. Salvation is put squarely in my own hands. My life is mine to live. Every choice leads either toward or away from *nirvana*. I am not the plaything of the Freudian unconscious, nor must I wait for divine grace from on high. Responsibility for salvation is mine alone. So the first two steps of the Eightfold Path call for intelligent properly motivated commitment.

Enlightenment doesn't come cheaply. Commitment must translate into action. "The man who talks much of the teaching but does not practice it himself is like a cowman counting another's cattle." Commitment finds expression in a moral life of "Right Speech" and "Right Action." If my commitment is truly compassionate, so will be my words. If my path is directed toward enlightenment, idle gossip and useless talk will have no place in my life. Silence rather than chatter is my norm (give away the transistor radios and TV sets). The fourth step of "Right Action" is the Keynote of the Eightfold Path. Buddhism focuses on Action, not Belief. So I must control anger (I will not kill), control desire for material things (I will not steal), control the lusts of the flesh (I will not act out of sensuality), control cowardice and malevolence (I will not lie), and control the craving for unwholesome excitement (I will not get drunk on intoxicating liquor or drugs). Note that these are not commandments demanding obedience to a power outside myself—"Thou shalt not." Rather they are a spelling out of the responsible commitment I take upon myself and make to myself. And these precepts apply to the mind as well as to the external deed. Slanderous, murderous, and lustful thoughts can be as harmful to myself and my victims as the overt acts. The mind can become drunk with excitement and distraction. And theft and injustice are not the less so because sanctioned by custom.

Through the practice of these precepts in thought and in deed, I am on my way to extinguish the craving (*trishna*) which is the source of anxiety and sorrow (*dukkha*). Not every way of life is compatible with this ideal, wherefore the fifth step in the Buddha's path is "Right Means of Livelihood." If the very way I earn my daily bread demands that I be caught up in a cycle of greed, deception, injustice, distraction, and "dog-eat-dog," how can I even enter upon the Buddha's path? I personally feel that this step is crucial for those who live in our western advertising/consumer-oriented war society. I suppose it is possible to play political, military, and Madison Avenue games with truthfulness, justice, chastity, compassion, and detachment from results, so no career should be condemned outright. But the Buddha's injunction is clear. If my occupation or trade forms an insuperable obstacle for *me*, then better I should change my occupation than abandon the Eightfold Path. How can a means of livelihood which brings anxiety and sorrow be preferred to a path which leads to *nirvana* and Enlightenment? It's a question of my hierarchy of values and the depth of my commitment to them.

Commitment expressed through moral action prepares me for the final three steps involving Meditation —"Right Effort," "Right Awareness" and "Right Concentration." "Right Effort" stresses the constant vigilance needed to remove from my life the cravings, compulsions, and habits that produce anxiety and sorrow. If you've ever tried to overcome even one minor bad habit, like smoking, from your life, you have a hint of what Right Effort entails. Contrary to its popular image, Buddhism is not for the passive and idle. Salvation does not drop from heaven. It is in my own hands. With Right Effort, I can practice "Right Awareness" and "Right Concentration"—practice, in other words, the Ways of Meditation outlined earlier in this book. The result for the Buddhist is enlightenment, the state of *nirvana*, when all craving, all sense of individual ego ceases in the surrender to the stream of Life and Becoming beyond all rationality and words. This is the final step of the Buddha's Eightfold Noble Path.

As soon as about one hundred years after the death of Gautama Buddha, Buddhism began to split into two parties or schools. The Buddhists of strict observance stressed the monastic and ascetical side of Buddhism. They claimed to follow the "Theravada," the Doctrine of the Elders, and laid great stress on the Ethical precepts of the Eightfold Path. This "straight and narrow" form of Buddhism came to be known, rather pejoratively, as *hinayana* ("the Lesser Vehicle") Buddhism, as opposed to *mahayana* ("the Greater Vehicle") Buddhism which arose in opposition to it. Buddhism for the masses could not be as strict as Buddhism confined to the monastery. The *hinayana* ideal of the *arhat* gave way to the *bodhisattva* ideal of *mahayana* Buddhism. The *arhat* or saint, unconcerned with others, strives for his own salvation and release. The *bodhisattva*, however, postpones the rewards of *nirvana* so that, out of his compassion for suffering humanity, he can bring the Buddha's truth to others. *Hinayana* was authoritarian and conservative, and stuck close to the canonical texts handed down by tradition. *Mahayana* was mystical and liberal, and tolerant of speculation and doctrinal development. *Hinayana* was a path of salvation through discipline for the few, whereas *mahayana* pointed out a path of devotion in everyday life for the masses.

These are not two Buddhisms. Both draw inspiration from Gautama, their founder. The differences between them are those of emphasis and psychology. *Hinayana* stressed morality and fidelity to the written teachings of the founder as codified in the "Ecumenical Councils" of the *theravada*. *Mahayana* stressed mysticism and devotion to the person of the Buddha rather than to his written code. This adaptability enabled Buddhism to spread throughout Asia as a truly catholic religion. And, paradoxically, this tolerance also led to its virtual disappearance from India, the country of its origin.

The word "Hindu" still means "Indian." It is a racial, cultural, social, and nationalistic term as well as religious. The pressures are overwhelmingly against the Indian who would live in India and not live as a Hindu. So it is not surprising that with the passage of time Hindu practices invaded the monasteries of *theravada* Buddhism. And it is even less surprising that *mahayana*, in its vast spirit of tolerance, eventually became indistinguishable from the Hindu way of life of the ordinary people. But the decline of Buddhism in India was matched by its missionary impulse which spread it to Ceylon, Burma, Siam, Cambodia, China, Korea, and Japan, in which countries it flourishes to the present day. These countries, in adopting Buddhism for themselves, infused and fertilized it with the spirit and genius peculiar to their own respective cultures. Later on, for example, we will see how Buddhism, transformed by its contact with Taoism in China, resulted in the unique Spirit of Zen Buddhism in Japan.

Before proceeding to the Taoist mystical tradition, let us recapitulate the Buddhist way of salvation.

The Buddhist Middle Way of the Fourfold Noble Truth contains a unique and essential insight for both the Christian and Humanist ways of salvation that characterize the western world. Buddhism, Christianity, and Humanism can each be viewed as a religion or way of salvation. In other words, each diagnoses the present state of mankind as an unhappy one. Each holds out a goal or ideal of happiness and salvation from this present human condition. And, finally, each presents a path leading to that goal. What indeed has the Buddhist with his agnosticism about God got to tell the Christian? Buddhism appears inimical to the two great western salvation systems, Christianity and Secular Humanism.

Secular Humanism focuses squarely on concrete empirical human existence. Death is not something to be lamented and overcome. Death is a fact to be faced without flinching and without mystical pretensions about escaping it. The world of reason, of time, of science, and of the sense is not illusion or the source of all our sorrow. This temporal world is the only world we have, and scientific reason is the unique tool that humans possess for dealing with this world. To the humanist, the ideal Buddhist *nirvana* might appear to be an evasion of the authentic responsibility of man "come of age" over his own destiny. And Buddhist mysticism might appear as the abdication of scientific reason which sets man apart from the rest of the universe.

Buddhism agrees with the humanist that salvation lies in man's own hands. Buddhism agrees with the Humanist that teachings and theories must be proved by the pragmatic test of life and experience. And it is precisely by such a pragmatic test that Humanist dogma is being shaken today. Ecological and military disasters raise the question that scientific reason has created not utopian man but a monster. Man has become afraid of man. Freed from the tyranny of gods and demons, secular man has become tyrant over himself.

It is at this point that the Christian points out the flaw in the Humanist and Buddhist paths. Salvation cannot come from human effort alone. No good will and no mere human striving suffices of itself. To be himself man must be open to what is more than himself. Both Humanism and Buddhism are wrong in not taking the transcendent positively into account. Reality is there for man to define, manipulate or withdraw from. But reality is more than human reality. It transcends man. Man must therefore be open to interventions of reality which he could never predict, expect, foresee, or control. However much as I would like to think that my salvific path lies in my own power, reality has some surprises for me. Man is more than man. He lives in a reality whose transcendent remains essentially mysterious. If he would be saved, he must keep open to this transcendent mystery. The doctrine of the Trinity is the Christian expression of this truth. Mankind and the universe is the Son of God coming to birth. By the incarnation we are brought into the realm of the divine. The Holy Spirit is the striving within us toward our mysterious transcendent Father. By the power of the Spirit (*Atman*) through our identity with the Son we keep open to the transcendent Father (*Brahman*).

Where Christianity points us toward transcendent mystery, Buddhism shows immanent mystery to both Christianity and Humanism. As transcendent reality has its surprises, immanent reality has its surprises too. This is what Buddhism tells us. Without the Buddhist insight, both scientific secularism and Christianity tend to be anti-human. Let's see how this is so.

First, the Buddhist mystic can caution the Christian that man may not legitimately be manipulated by the "Will of God." Despite the current stress on "Humanistic Christianity" we cannot ignore the long series of anti-human episodes in the history of Christianity. In time of war, for example, the will of my nation, my little piece of turf, is alleged to be the will of the great transcendent divinity, and so I march off to kill in the name of God. The United States aircraft carrier Forrestal has a stained-glass window on its chapel depicting the outstretched hand of God shooting forth jet bombers on their murderous missions. And the belt buckles of Nazi soldiers in World War II were engraved with the motto "For God and Country." No need to mention the preachers down through the centuries condemning alcohol, gambling, smoking, fornicating, sexual thoughts, bad books, dancing, eating meat, Sunday morning lay-abeds, all in the name of God. The alleged "Will of God," backed up by inquisition, the stake, excommunication, heaven and hell, has been invoked to manipulate men even to the most secret recesses of their thoughts. The Buddhist path exposes these "divine" precepts and condemnations for what they are—human constructs. Neither God, nor man, nor expectations concerning human behavior, meaning, or goals can be successfully captured and defined in our rational and religious categories. To cling to these categories and expectations is *trishna*. The result is sorrow, the cure is *nirvana*, letting go, surrendering to the immanent mystery human life which is more than my little rational mind ever dreamed of.

The Buddhist mystic also corrects the excessive rationalism of the secular humanist. The intimate friendship of humanism and science is breaking down. We are succumbing to what is horrifyingly called "The Technological Imperative": "Whatever technology *can* do, technology *ought* to do." Technology *can* produce poison gas, genocidal bacteria, test-tube babies, cloned zygotes, and cobalt bombs. Therefore it *ought* to produce all these things. Technology *can* eavesdrop on all our phone calls, computerize all our financial transactions, program everyone into his most appropriate slot in the industrial machine. Therefore technology *ought* to do all these things. Buddhism calls a halt to the manipulation of man in the name of scientific reason. To cling to the ideals of scientific rationality is *trishna*. The result is sorrow, the suffocating sense of anxiety and helplessness we are experiencing today in the western world. The cure is *nirvana*, letting go, allowing human reality to develop in ways that scientific reason never dreamed of. Neither religion nor science can box in or define the immanent mystery of human existence. The mystic state of *nirvana* for all its apparent emptiness is the fullest kind of living. It is empty only of the human categories that would restrict it. The resultant enlightenment cannot be spoken of, but only lived. This is where the Buddha's Fourfold Noble Truth was meant to lead us all.

If you find the Buddhist world a friendly place to be,

you may find the Taoist world even friendlier. At any rate, our next stop is China and the Taoist interpretation of mystical experience.

MICHIO KUSHI—MACROBIOTIC TEACHER. SYMBOLS ON BLACK-BOARD ILLUSTRATE THE ORDER OF THE UNIVERSE—A CONTEMPORARY WAY OF LIFE BASED ON THE ANCIENT PRINCIPLES OF THE TAO.

Photo by Ivan Spane.

VII
Taoism

Taoism is at once the most mystical and the most revolutionary philosophy in the history of mankind. It has a long and bizarre history dating from its origins in primitive rural religion which crystallized into a mystical philosophy, a philosophy which later took a turn toward magic and alchemy, and became on and off the officially recognized state religion. We focus on the mystical and philosophical side of Taoism. It is this dimension of Taoism that continues to have the greatest impact on the West. It is the Taoism of the formative years of the fifth century B.C., expressed in the teachings of Lao Tzu and of his popularizer, Chuang Tzu.

Some similarities will appear between Taoism and Buddhism, but it is more enlightening to consider their great differences. Buddhism is a religion with an historical founder. Taoism is a way of looking at the world. It has a spokesman in the shadowy figure of Lao Tzu, but he is not properly the "founder" or originator of this world view. Buddhism preaches compassion and salvation, whereas Taoism does not enjoin action for the benefit of others—quite the opposite. Buddhism is psychological, starting inside with an analysis of mind. Taoism is cosmological, focusing outward on an attitude toward Nature. In spite of mutual influences that were to blossom into Zen in Japan, Buddhism as transplanted into China from India remained incompatible with and in opposition to Taoist doctrines.

We start with a man who may never have existed, Lao Tzu (Lao pronounced like the first three letters of "louse"; Tzu is a short buzzing sound), and a book he may never have written, *Tao Te Ching* (pronounced *dow der jing*). Concerning Lao Tzu (which means Old Boy) we have nothing but legend to go on. He is said to have been born sometime in the sixth century B.C. Confucius is said to have visited him and gone away baffled. After Lao Tzu wrote the classic *Tao Te Ching*, tradition has it that he went off to the West. No one knows how or when he died. In any case, we do have a book, the *Tao Te Ching*. Someone or many people wrote it. In lieu of other available names, we might as well refer to the author as Lao Tzu.[1]

Tao can be translated "the Way." *Te* means "Virtue" in the sense of "Power." *Ching* means "Classic." *Tao Te Ching*, therefore, is translated as the Classic of the Way and the Power. As is the case in every mystical philosophy, Taoism defies rational verbal explanations. Having said that, we will now proceed with an attempt at verbalizing the essential doctrines of the *Tao Te Ching*. This doctrine revolves around four key notions, namely, (1) *wu wei* (the doctrine of "inaction"), (2) *te* (virtue or power), (3) *p'u* (the teaching about one's "original self"), and (4) *tao* (the mysterious and elusive notion of "the Way").

First, the doctrine of "inaction." *Wu wei* literally means "not doing." What is the secret of power and effectiveness in life? Lao Tzu's paradoxical and possibly exasperating answer is *wu wei*. The secret of doing is not doing. The best way of controlling the actions of others is to do nothing about them. Let's see what this means.

Try to kill a bee, and you'll get stung. Throw a punch, and you'll be punched back. Humiliate an employee, and he will await his day of revenge. In human affairs, force is counterproductive. It defeats itself. Challenge an animal, a man, or a nation, and you are going to call forth a response. That is why there will never be a war to end all wars. In the very act of victory I plant the seed for the next war. The harder I try to bend another to my will, the more vigorous will be his resistance. And conversely, if I am challenged, but refuse to respond, the challenge fizzles. You can't have a fight without an antagonist. It takes two. The Taoist turns the other cheek not because it's a pious and virtuous thing to do, but because this way of acting (not acting) is effective. *Wu wei* is a pragmatic doctrine.

Wu wei works because it cuts much more deeply than mere action. *Wu wei* is an attitude, a way of *being*. I don't futilely try to *compel* another by action. Rather I *attract* him by my attitude and very being. By love and compassion, I cause the other to want what I want. If I am humble and compassionate, the other has no cause to fear me, no reason to put me down. It's my attitude, not my action, that determines the response of others. One teacher can silence a noisy classroom with a glance, whereas for another, scolding and even punishments don't work.

To practice *wu wei* is not to become a doormat. The doormat personality is completely ineffectual. He yields his very being and attitudes to the enemy, and thereby encourages opposition. On the other hand, the Taoist does not oppose the "enemy" even wordlessly. If someone senses opposition in my attitude, he is going to become all the more determined to oppose me. The Taoist knows that in human relations, resistance begets resistance. *Wu wei*, then, is neither a yielding to opposition nor a resisting of it. How is this possible? The answer lies in the Taoist's complete relativism.

The Taoist adopts the other man's opinion as his own, without judging it as good or bad. This refusal to set up rules for doing good is where Lao Tzu differs most radically from Confucius. A standard of good implies a standard of evil. This leads to fighting evil. And fighting evil makes evil grow stronger. Resistance begets resistance. So when I run into a man who would oppose me, I enter into his point of view. After all, his perspective is as valid as mine. It has its own truth just as my perspective has *its* own. Milk is good for your health, says the American Dairy Association. But a Chinaman becomes physically nauseous at the sight of an adult drinking milk. What a pacifist calls murder, a bomber pilot calls patriotism. And so it goes.

It's impossible to tell *the* truth to a Taoist. Every truth is incomplete, and so is partly false as well. True and false, like good and evil, are complementary opposites. They beget each other, imply each other. Such is the doctrine of *yin* and *yang* which we'll see later in the chapter. So it's also impossible to tell a lie to a Taoist. He will sense the truth behind the lie. When I lie to my Taoist girl friend that I make $25,000 a year, she senses that I'm telling her, "I want you to think that I am an important, wealthy and admirable person." So it is not hypocrisy when the Taoist takes on the opinion and viewpoint of his would-be enemy.

So *wu wei* is neither a yielding to nor a resisting of the would-be enemy. Rather *wu wei* disarms the enemy by entering into his point of view, putting oneself in his shoes. You've done this yourself, haven't you? How do you silence a belligerent drunk? Agree with him. How do you appease your upset wife? Repeat her argument accurately and compassionately, thereby showing how you sympathize thoroughly with her point of view. These are homely everyday applications of Lao Tzu's doctrine of actionless activity, doing without doing. In a word, "The way to do is to be." Closely connected with this is the second key notion of the *Tao Te Ching*, namely, the concept of *te*.

Te means "virtue" or "power." *Te* is what you get from the practice of *wu wei*. *Te* is your deepest principle of harmony. *Tao*, as we will see, refers to order and harmony in Nature, the macrocosm. *Te* is the microcosmic principle of order and harmony. *Te* is the power that comes to a man who through the practice of *wu wei* has put himself in harmony with the *tao*, with the order of Nature. *Te* is a mystical state, a state of enlightenment. Through the practice of contemplation, the man of *te* has quieted his mind. He has moved from the realm of action to that of not-doing, of actionless activity.

The practice of *wu wei* and the resultant power or *te* involves an inner transformation, a new way of being. *Wu wei* involves a letting go of preconceived man-made order, social conventions, rigid concepts. The *tao* refuses to be frozen or grasped. But when by contemplation I achieve utter harmonious spontaneity, then I am in tune with the harmonious spontaneity of all things. I am in tune with the *tao*. The man of *te* has his great power because he is plugged into the orderly energy of the cosmos itself. Indeed, the artificial distinction between the individual self and Nature breaks down. "The world is my body." Chapter 16 of the *Tao Te Ching* enumerates the stages of contemplation through which this identification takes place:

The all-changing changeless is all-embracing;
To embrace all is to be selfless.
To be selfless is to be all-pervading.
To be all-pervading is to be transcendent.[2]

    Te is a well-nigh infinite power.

    So *te* is a profound and mysterious force. The enlightened man is more than an expert in social engineering, getting others to want what he wants through *wu wei*. *Te* is a moral force, a kind of charism. It is a personal power that comes as a result of being in tune with the *tao*. *Te* is my *karma*, not a *karma* to be worked out at some future life or time, but a *karma* whose impact is *now*. Not what I have *done* in the past, but who I *am* now, this is what gives me power. This is *te*. *Te* shines out from my character, from my very being. *Te* flows from my uncorrupted self, my spontaneous self, the self that is in tune with the law of all things, i.e., with the *tao*.

    Like other mystical traditions Taoism recognizes that most of us are not in touch with the being that we truly are. Most of us fail to tap this great resource we possess. *Te* is at once supremely simple and extremely difficult to obtain. *Te* is simply my ability to follow my own nature. The lion roaming through the jungle has *te*. With this compare the caged lion withering away in the zoo. In the jungle the lion is able to behave in accordance with its own nature. Most of us have lost touch with our own original natures. We are unable to move so freely and spontaneously. Society has become our zoo. We wither away in our artificial cages.

    Not only do I tend to deviate from my own way, from my own particular nature, but I tend to want to make other people deviate from their own paths. The teacher who demands conformity, the parent who would make his child over into his own image, the congressman who would legislate morality, all these are examples of how we stifle *te* in others. That is why Lao Tzu says there is no greater evil than the desire to change others. For Confucius, if we each follow our raw original natures, society becomes impossible. Nature requires an overlay of the spontaneous rites and conventions of social life if society is to be possible. Lao Tzu is more optimistic. Evil comes not from failure to conform to convention, ritual, and law. No, law, convention, morality are what precisely create evil. For these suppress the great natural power of *te* that strives to be born in each one of us. This is why I have called Taoism the most revolutionary philosophy in the history of mankind. It calls for an absolute minimum of government, law, and morality. It is sheer anarchy. But the anarchy brought about by this subversion of law, morality, and government is not chaos. Anarchy is saved from chaos by the universal law of spontaneous harmony in individual *te* and cosmic *tao*.

It is clear, then, how closely *te* is related to the third key notion in the *Tao Te Ching*, namely, the concept of *p'u*, one's "natural self," one's "original nature." One who practices *wu wei* has *te* because he has returned to *p'u*, his original uncorrupted self. *P'u* means "plain" in modern Chinese. Originally it meant "wood" straight from the tree before it has been carved or shaped by man. The *Tao Te Ching* also speaks of one's original self under the metaphor of Raw Silk that has never been painted or dyed, or of the Newborn Child in his native simplicity before society has trained or molded him. The child fresh from the womb is naturally good until it becomes twisted and corrupted by society. The enlightened man is one who has become as a child again.

Aggression, ambition, competition, greediness are all taught by society. A multitude of desires are implanted in us which guarantees that we will be forever unsatisfied. What is Lao Tzu's prescription? Go to a forest or walk along a beach and pick up an uncarved piece of wood, *p'u*, and hold it in your hand. Admire the simplicity, feel the plainness, get a sense of your own original nature. Through quiet and contemplation, acquire the habit of *wu wei*. Return to your pristine innocence, to "fewness of desires." This is not a Chinese form of Christian asceticism urging us to root out carnal desires. The Taoist does not see the flesh as the chief enemy of progress in the spirit. Spirit and flesh are not distinguished and opposed. Indeed the unspoiled self is one with itself and with Nature. The original self's fleshly desires are few and good. The desires that Lao Tzu bids us root out are the desires that society has added to those original few such as the lust after money and power and status and importance. The effort to satisfy these desires is diametrically opposed to the law of *wu wei*. And since effort and aggression beget counter efforts and counter aggression, all my striving is bound to recoil on itself and fail. Thus I am led further and further away from my original nature. And so the return to "fewness of desires" is essential to the discovery of *p'u*, from which flows power or *te*.

But note, I should not become attached to or selfishly preoccupied with acquiring *te*. The man of *te* has great power to move and influence others, but he does not seek *te in order to* be able to control others. His desire to control will be sensed by others and hence will defeat itself. *Te*, like happiness, comes to those who do not seek it directly. Otherwise I fall into the trap of the man who is humble and proud of it. Action is not the way to actionless activity. Rather, *wu wei* is the way to *wu wei*.

The state of original innocence or *p'u* cuts more deeply still. Not only do I discard desire for money, power, and status. I also discard law, duty, morality, and the distinction of right from wrong! These all are society's efforts to distort and corrupt the purity of *p'u*, my original nature. In the attitude of *wu wei* not only do I refrain from trying to dominate others, but I also ignore the attempts of others to dominate me however much these attempts be cloaked in the mantle of law, morality, and goodness. Lao Tzu does not hesitate to draw these subversive and radical conclusions that are inherent in all mysticisms. Because of his insight the mystic asserts the claim to be beyond good and evil, beyond conventional morality and socially applied laws. Again, this anarchy does not lead to chaos. If I do not allow violence to be done to me even in the name of God, then I will not be inclined to do violence to others. To live in touch with *p'u* is to live in original innocence in harmony with myself, Nature, and all things. "Banish wisdom, discard knowledge, and the people will be benefited a hundredfold: banish human kindness, discard morality, and the people will be dutiful and compassionate." The Taoist, however, does not flaunt his *p'u*, or glory in his amorality. This would be contrary to the spirit of *wu wei* and would only provoke opposition and violence. He keeps his own counsel. He lives in the world of conventions and laws but is not of that world.

The Taoist, then, is not a "do-gooder." This does not mean that he doesn't do good. The Taoist would never lead a band of white suburbanites, as a Christian pastor did recently, on a Sunday expedition into the heart of Harlem to clean up the streets. But he certainly would follow the natural compassionate promptings of his *p'u* to aid a man who called to him in need. The man of *te* acts out of a harmonious spontaneity and not out of the dictates of a formal morality. His path is not the rigid one staked out by society. He follows his own path, his own Way. This Way works for him because it is in harmony with the Way or the *tao* of all things. We are ready now to look at this fourth and most important notion in the *Tao Te Ching*, namely, the concept of *tao*.

We have implied, and now we explicitly state, that Taoism is more than just an ethics. Taoism is at heart a metaphysics, a way of looking at the universe. For the Greeks the universe was a "cosmos," an orderly whole. For the Taoist, too, there is a universal harmony that rules all things. That universal harmony is the *tao*. *Tao* can be translated as Nature. Or better, *tao* means the "Way," i.e., the Way of Nature, the Way or Path that all things follow when they are true to themselves.

What precisely is this Way, this *tao?* Now we enter the realm of mystery. Such a question seeks the secret of Being and asks that that secret be spelled out in words. The wise man through contemplation and *wu wei* can discover his original nature which is in tune with the *tao*, but the *tao* cannot be named or conceptualized or put into words. The mystic who lives at the heart of Ultimate Reality is rendered speechless. "Those who know do not speak; those who speak do not know," says Lao Tzu.

Lao Tzu, in the manner of other mystical traditions, does tell us what the *tao* is *not*.

There was something formlessly fashioned,
That existed before heaven and earth;
Without sound, without substance,
Dependent on nothing, unchanging,
All pervading, unfailing.
One may think of it as the mother of all things under
    heaven.
Its true name we do not know;
"Way" (*tao*) is the by-name we give it.[3]

Like Christians and Hindus, Lao Tzu has a double way
of referring to the *tao* or Ultimate Reality. For Christians God is at once immanent in the universe and tran-
scendentally beyond and incomparable to it. The Vedantist speaks of "manifest" Brahman pervading
everything we know, and secret inaccessible "hidden"
Brahman. Lao Tzu speaks of nameable *tao* that is the
mother and the Way of all things, and the "Something
Else" from which this *tao* arose. This "Something
Else" is referred to as the Self-So, the Nameless, and
even Non-Being.

The *tao* that can be *tao'd* is not the Absolute *tao*
The name that can be named is not the absolute name.[4]

If the sum of all we can possibly experience is Being,
then call that Something Else on which Being depends
"Non-Being." It is utterly incomparable to anything we
can know. If we give names to all the beings of the universe and their patterns and harmonies, then that on
which they depend is the Nameless. The manifest *tao* is
Being, the One, the great mother, the Way and the harmony in which all opposites are reconciled. The hidden
aspect of *tao* is Non-Being, the Nameless, the Something Else from which all things arise.

What does *tao* do? We most readily experience the *tao* in the relentless irresistible Order of Nature. *Tao* is not a personal God. *Tao* plays no favorites. *Tao* is impersonal and dispassionate. Each being does best by following its own uncorrupted nature which reflects the law of *tao*. Attempts to change my nature, to follow the beat of a drummer who is not my own, will backfire. *Tao* cannot be thwarted. Season must follow upon season. The sprout grows into the plant which matures and then must wither and die. Such is the Way, the *tao*. It is the *tao* that rains upon just and unjust alike, that clothes the lilies of the field, and sees them shrivel up and die. Each thing is best at being what it is. A dog does poorly walking on its hind legs as does a man on all fours. *Te* is the power of the *tao*. *Wu wei* is the attribute of the *tao*. *P'u* is the reflection of the *tao*. The *tao* pervades all things but cannot be grasped. It is utterly simple, and utterly elusive. The *tao* is the will of all things, yet it has no will of its own. An eighth-century Chinese verse captures this elusive pervasive quality of the *tao* by the metaphor of a reflected image:

The wild geese fly across the long sky above.
Their image is reflected upon the chilly water below.
The geese do not mean to cast their image upon the water;
Nor does water mean to hold the image of the geese.[5]

So much for Lao Tzu, the originator of Taoism's mystical tradition.

Chuang Tzu was Lao Tzu's most prominent follower and did most to popularize the doctrines of the *Tao Te Ching*. His writings were much more exuberant and poetic than those of his master. Only one biographical detail about him survives. The King of Ch'u, hearing of

Chuang Tzu's talent, sent a messenger to him with rich gifts and an invitation to become a minister in the palace. Chuang Tzu just laughed. "You want to deck me out in fine clothes and fatten me up like an ox led to sacrifice. I'd rather be an unknown piglet wallowing in the mire free to live as I will." The fall of the mighty from power is a constant theme in his work. Because they ignore the law of actionless activity the powerful fall into the traps that they set for others.

The successful ruler is a mystic. He must govern by not governing. Indeed Taoist teaching is aimed especially at the king. In the king above all the power of *te* should show forth. All the king need do if he would govern successfully is look after the *tao*. It's something like Jesus said, "Seek ye first the kingdom of God and all other things shall be yours as well." The Taoist ruler is not an absolute pacifist who rejects all use of force. Nor is he a militarist making the world safe for democracy or anything else. If a man invaded his home and attacked his family, he doubtless would use force against the attacker, but he would use it reluctantly. And this reluctance would be sensed by the intruder. It would not be the kind of force that begets even further aggression. The ideal Taoist ruler is a mystic, but he's not unrealistic. As a matter of fact he is a mystic precisely because this is the most effective, pragmatic and realistic way of ruling.

The dogmatic one-sided desire to impose their will on others is why rulers usually cause wars rather than peace and prosperity. The Taoist ruler however knows that all opinions are both true and false, and that all actions are both good and evil. While the rest of men spin round and round in mindless activity like the spokes of a wheel, the Taoist is serenely quiet at the hub. However absurd his subjects' whims, he does not quarrel with them. He is like the monkey trainer, says Chuang Tzu, who had to cut down on his animals' food. "You'll get three pieces in the morning," the trainer told the monkeys, "and four at night." The monkeys were furious. "All right," he said. "You can have four pieces in the morning and three at night." The monkeys were delighted. The Taoist ruler has no preferences, since he knows that any preference of his own would be just as arbitrary as the preferences opposed to it would be.

The wise ruler does not seek to help, instruct, or convert his subjects. His government is "laissez faire" in the sense of *wu wei*. The wise man is not useful for others. A tree has a chance of growing tall and strong, says Chuang Tzu, only if it is useless to the carpenter. But if the wood is fine and the grain is straight, the carpenter will cut it up into planks. We know how to be useful, but we don't understand the value of being useless. This is so true of technological society. The productive citizen we reward. But the old and the defective we want to either do away with or hide away. Of course, useful and useless are opposite sides of the same coin. The wise man is as useful and as useless as the *tao*. The doctrine of *yin* and *yang*, the identity of opposites, governs all things.

The realization of *yin* and *yang* causes the Taoist to be utterly serene in the face of death. The change from life to death is as natural as the change from day to night, waking to sleeping, summer to winter. Animals and plants die that I might eat and live. I die that they might live. At his death Chuang Tzu's disciples wanted to give him a great funeral. Here is what he said:

"Heaven and earth are my coffin and my grave; for

burial regalia I will have the sun and the moon as my double jade ring, the stars as my jewels. . . . What would you add to this?"

The disciples replied, "We fear that you may be eaten by the crows and kites."

Chuang Tzu replied, "Above ground, I will be eaten by the crows and kites; below, I will be eaten by the crickets and ants. Why rob one to feed the other?"[6]

The doctrine of *yin* and *yang* so beautifully applied here to the acceptance of life and death has its origin in the *I Ching*, the Book of Changes. We will conclude this chapter with some remarks on this ancient mysterious book which was the main source of inspiration for both Lao Tzu and Confucius. Throughout Chinese history as well as today in the West, the *I Ching* is popular as a book of magical divination. It is, however, more profoundly a book of Wisdom, and this is how we will treat it here. The *I Ching* is about change. Its fundamental premise is that change makes sense. Change has its own rhythm and law. In the *I Ching* is developed the law of the *tao* which is the doctrine of "opposites," a doctrine which came to be known as that of *yang* and *yin*. The *yin-yang* doctrine does not explain change by means of causality as modern science does. No. The *yin-yang* doctrine is explanation by way of "synchronicity" as psychoanalyst C. G. Jung has pointed out. Let's look at the meaning of *yin* and *yang* and of synchronicity.[7]

The law of the *tao* is the law of identity of opposites, i.e., the law of oneness in duality. The spontaneous change of the *tao* is governed by the pulsating rhythm of those two alternating primal states of being, *yang* and *yin*. The original meaning of *yang* is "sunshiny." *Yin* originally meant "cloudy." These were extended to

mean the "bright" and the "shady" sides of a mountain, and thence to all opposing pairs such as the mas-
culine and the feminine, life and death, day and night,
summer and winter, etc. Whatever happens in the world
arises from this interplay of opposites. At any given instant of my life certain *yang* forces and/or certain *yin*
forces are prevailing in my particular situation. And
out of these interplaying forces some are more crucial
than others. If I could tap the secret of the particular
confluence of forces playing upon me at this instant,
then I might know the most favorable way to respond
in order to keep in tune with the *tao*. I would receive *te*
because I would be locked into the particular combination of *yang* and *yin* forces influencing me at the moment. The interplay of *yang* and *yin*, you recall, is the
Law of the *tao*. The *I Ching*, then, not only states the
Law of the *tao*, but gives me a method for bringing my
life under the influence of that supreme law.

The method of consulting the *I Ching* bears some re-
semblance to consulting your horoscope or to opening
your Bible at random in search of advice. By tossing
coins (or yarrow stalks) you are referred to the section
of the *I Ching* that is supposed to describe the particular combination of *yang* and *yin* forces operating on
you at that instant. Before dismissing as superstitious
such a random or chance method of consulting *The
Book of Changes* (or the Bible!), consider that there
may be more than a grain of truth here. I might like to
think that I have an orderly rational life governed by
fairly predictable laws. But the unpredictable is at least
as important as the predictable. Chance plays as much
a part in my life as does law. In fact, it is precisely by
ignoring chance that scientific laws are derived. Science
operates under laboratory conditions. The "variables"

(i.e., the chance random factors) are "controlled." But I don't live any life under laboratory conditions. Unpredictable variables hit one on all sides and can profoundly affect my life in ways totally unforeseen. Consider the "chance" meeting that blossoms into a marriage, the "accident" that breaks my leg, the "coincidence" when a daughter has the same birthday that her mother has. Life is a series of accidents, variables, and coincidences, some trivial and unnoticed, others remarkable and startling.

We in the West like to explain things by their causes. The present, we feel, was caused by forces operating in the past. When I can point to the past causes, then the present "makes sense." Otherwise it is a "coincidence." The Chinese view it differently. "Coincidence" is what makes sense. The present is the cause of the present. I am what I am now, not so much because of what has happened in the past, but because of what is happening *now*. Each situation is unique. At each instant all the *yin-yang* forces of the *tao* are mutually influencing each other. Everything is related to everything else. When I toss the coins to consult the *I Ching*, I am taking a barometer reading of the cosmic weather at this particular instant. What I find is as much of a question of my own state of mind as it is of what is written in the book. After all, I too am part of that cosmic play of forces. What is primary is not causality operating in the past but the coincident simultaneous play of *yin-yang* forces operating in the present. This latter is what C. G. Jung calls "synchronicity." *Yin-yang* influences change from moment to moment. The *Book of Changes*, then, is a compilation of the various combinations that *yin-yang* influences can take as moment follows moment in my life.

There are two ways in which I can consult the *Book of Changes* to discover the coincident forces operating on me at this instant. First, I can do it superstitiously and magically: toss the coins and accept literally the "answer" that I am referred to in the *I Ching*. This would be much like accepting the daily newspaper's horoscope as the guide of my life. The *I Ching* would be viewed as a book of divination. But I can approach it, too, as a book of wisdom. In this spirit I prepare myself before I read, entering by meditation into harmony with the *tao* as far as I can. Both my spirit of contemplation and the words of the *I Ching* will enter into my reading and interpretation. This approach is like a Christian opening a Bible at random to read in a spirit of prayer and trust. In any case, from the time of Lao Tzu's ancestors down through to the present, the *I Ching* has had an abiding influence on all who would seek harmony with the *tao*, whether they approached it in a spirit of magic or in a spirit of contemplation.

This book's teachings are a particularly effective antidote for the poisons of the industrial western world. In the West, as Herbert Marcuse has pointed out, we are enslaved by "technological rationality." In other words, man has become the servant of the needs of technology rather than technology's being the servant of the needs of man. Technology tries to reduce our lives to the antiseptic conditions of the vast laboratory which is the economy. We are pressured into suppressing those parts of our lives which do not fit into the computer, the assembly line, or the sales graph. It would like to reduce us completely to being mere cogs in the wheels of production and garbage pails of consumption. And why? Because it is good for us as human beings? No. It is "good for the economy."

Lao Tzu and Chuang Tzu in the tradition of the *I Ching* teach us that man is governed by more than scientific laws and rational patterns. All the chances, coincidences, and unpredictable spontaneities of the present are part of man's full reality. It is man's destiny to resonate with the All, with the *yin-yang* rhythms of the *tao*. Life and death are reverse sides of the same coin. Technology's efforts to repress death are madness. Individual and society are two perspectives on the same reality. Cut-throat competition pitting individual against individual is equally madness and literally suicidal. Good and evil imply each other. To pit the virtuous man against the criminal is madness, too. It stifles the good in the criminal and blinds the virtuous man to the evil in his own heart. Western man tends to polarize opposites and set them at each other's throats. The eastern mystic fuses them. He knows that *yin* and *yang* go hand in hand, for such is the law of the *tao*.

This law of the *tao* inspired Lao Tzu and Chung Tzu to formulate that doctrine so subversive to western ways of thinking. The wise man aims not at busyness but at *wu wei*, not at manipulating others but at *te*, not at civilization but at *p'u*. Stop activity! Stop helping others! Stop progress! These three maxims alone show how the quiet Taoist mystic can be viewed with alarm as a radical revolutionary. He strikes at western man's most sacred and unquestioned dogmas.

Would I have to become a dropout from western society if I were to incorporate Taoist attitudes into my way of life? I think not. The *wu wei* injunction to "stop activity" is not a counsel of inaction. *Wu wei* means actionless *activity*. The Taoist still involves himself in the world's events, but his involvement is much more subtle than that of the technocrat who would try to dominate reality by the sheer force of energy. He controls events by getting in tune with them rather than by attempting to force the direction of their flow. Lao Tzu and Chuang Tzu were not addressing potential dropouts. In fact their writings were addressed primarily to the king so that he might become through the practice of Taoist mysticism a master in the art of governing and a model for all his subjects.

Wu wei does not emasculate its practitioner. Rather it is a source of power. It gives him *te*. The man of *te* is much more in control of his relationships to others than is the domineering man. Aggression begets counter-aggression. Domination arouses resistance. *Te* is power precisely because it does not seek power. It works by attraction, not by aggression. Because it does not seek to help others, others are left freer to help themselves.

The man of *te* has power because he is in tune with his original nature, with *p'u*. The Taoist condemns progress not out of perversity, but because what seems to be progress is not progress at all. With Rousseau, Freud, and Marcuse, the Taoist sees civilization as a process of decline. The appearance of progress is merely the substitution of new evils for the old. My original nature is good. It is perverted by the gadgetry of civilization and by the blindness enforced by education which inculcates the false ideals of busyness, competition and progress. These false ideals blind me to *p'u* whose true power is *te* and whose true progress is the practice of *wu wei*.

This power and this progress are firmly based in the *tao*, the Way. If through the practice of Taoist mysticism my individual path comes to tread in the Way of All Things, how can I fail? Such is the characteristic

Chinese insight into mystical experience. The Taoist view found its way over to Japan—not, however, Taoism in its pure form but rather in a curious marriage with Buddhism. The result is Zen.

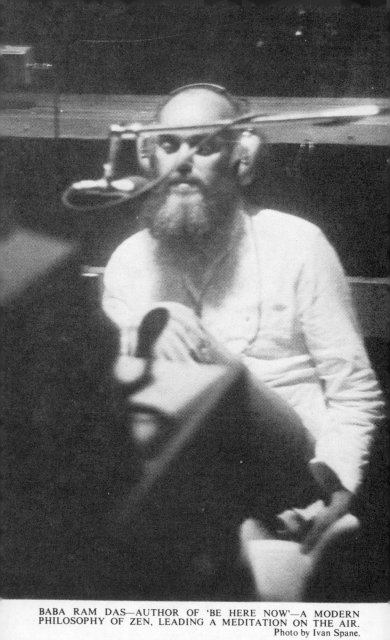

BABA RAM DAS—AUTHOR OF 'BE HERE NOW'—A MODERN
PHILOSOPHY OF ZEN, LEADING A MEDITATION ON THE AIR.
Photo by Ivan Spane.

VIII
Zen

No man has done more to popularize Zen in the West than Daisetz Taitaro Suzuki. His books together with the prolific outpourings of Alan Watts have presented to the English-speaking world a version of Zen as an experience which lies beyond all possible categories and criticism. Zen, we are told, is without doctrine and without philosophy.[1] It transcends space and time and cultures. Recent studies are showing up Suzuki's approach as pure and gratuitous mystification. Zen is being returned to the realm of the human again, a realm, incidentally, where our chance of successfully dipping into its riches is greatly enhanced. Zen has a human father in Buddhism and a human mother in Taoism. The history of Zen has been directed by outstanding human personages. There is Bodhidharma, the shadowy Indian patriarch, who brought Buddhism into China. There is Dogen, the founder of the *Soto* sect of Zen in Japan. There is the great modern Zen Master Hakuin, whose renewal of the *Rinzai* sect has been responsible for the resurgence of Zen in the Japan of today. Indeed, what could be more human than that Zen should have broken up into two opposing sects, the *Soto* and the *Rinzai*, with their respectively different approaches to enlightenment. And there is the great artist Matsuo Basho, who developed the exquisitely delicate *haiku* form of poetry to express his Zen enlightenment. We will trace this course of the evolution of Zen

in hopes of getting a feel for its beauty and richness
along the way.

The flow of Buddhism into China began as early as
the first century A.D. and by the fourth century it was
well established there. Along with their other doctrines
the Buddhists brought their teachings on *meditation
(dhyana)*. This Sanskrit term in Chinese was rendered
Ch'an, which in Japanese became *Zen.* Indian Buddhism quickly became naturalized Chinese, especially
through its contacts with Taoism. Of course, many
Buddhists resisted this indigenization and to that extent
found themselves persecuted and at odds with the local
culture. We need not look far to see the basis of this incompatibility. Buddhist monasticism and the Indian
tendency to flee from the world and nature was opposed to the Chinese attitude fostering close family ties
and harmony with the world and nature. But Buddhism's mystical bent and its tolerance in the interpretation of doctrine led it to be increasingly assimilated to
the interpretation and attitudes of Taoist mysticism.
This Buddhist-Taoist amalgam is what resulted in Zen.

It was the Taoist focus on nature and on mysticism
that made it fertile soil for Buddhism. Buddhist categories quickly found Taoist equivalents. In Mahayana
Buddhism the Buddha had taken on cosmic dimensions
much like the cosmic Christ of St. Paul who exists at
the heart of all things. This glorified cosmic Buddha
became the *tao.* The Buddhist Middle Path was assimilated to the Chinese *wu wei.* The primal nothingness of
nirvana was related to the non-being of nameless *tao.*
And each man's Buddha-nature was assimilated to the
Taoist *p'u* or original nature. This Buddha-nature of
all sentient beings is utterly simple and without com-
plication and for that reason completely elusive and

not explicable in words and categories. You either experience it through mystical enlightenment or you don't. Enlightenment becomes an all or nothing affair. The path to enlightenment may be long and rugged, but when enlightenment comes it is instantaneous. This doctrine of instantaneous enlightenment took root early in the history of Chinese Buddhism and became a primary characteristic of Zen, especially in the *Rinzai* sect.

Aside from the Buddha himself, the most revered figure in the Zen tradition is Bodhidharma.[2] The last of twenty-eight Buddhist patriarchs who trace themselves back to the Buddha himself, Bodhidharma came from the West from India to become the first patriarch of Chinese Zen. His coming to China from the West is an event revered by Zennists almost as the coming of Christ is revered by Christians. Countless Zen sutras begin with the question, "What is the meaning of Bodhidharma's coming from the West?" This question became a synonym for asking "What is the meaning of Zen?"

Bodhidharma's life is shrouded in legend. He definitely existed and was a native of India. Far from being unconcerned with its historical origins as Suzuki implies, Zennists proclaimed that theirs was the authentic teaching of the Buddha himself. The figure of Bodhidharma provides that authentic link to India for Buddhism now transplanted to a foreign land. Bodhidharma worked mainly in northern China during the first half of the sixth century A.D. The most famous monastery associated with his name is Shao-lin-ssu on Mount Sung. It is here that Bodhidharma is said to have seated himself staring at a wall in uninterrupted meditation for nine years until his legs withered away. Thus the first patriarch of Chinese Zen instituted that new path to enlightenment, *za-zen* ("sitting-meditation") that was to become a characteristic part of the Zen tradition. This "wall-gazing" type of meditation has a symbolic dimension too. The wall refers to the steepness and suddenness of enlightenment. As pointed out above, instantaneous enlightenment, too, peculiarly characterizes the Zen tradition of Buddhism. The doctrine of *za-zen* and of *gradual* enlightenment became a mark of the *Soto* sect of Zen. And the doctrine of instantaneous enlightenment and the use of the *koan* was stressed by the *Rinzai* sect of Zen. Both of these opposing sects could claim Bodhidharma, and through him the Buddha, as their Master.

The *Rinzai* (*Lin-chi* in Chinese) branch of Zen (*Ch'an* in Chinese) Buddhism was the closer of the two to Taoism. These devotees of instant enlightenment delighted in paradox, mistrusted books and words, stressed active personal encounter with the Master rather than long sitting meditations, relied on intuition often with humor rather than tedious logical argumentation, and felt that close communion with nature was the atmosphere best conducive to enlightenment. This whole spirit is captured in the use of the *koan*, those maddening typically Zen riddles of which we will see more below, as a technique for triggering the immediate experience of enlightenment. The *Ts'ao-tung (Soto)* branch of *Ch'an* Buddhism was more conservative. They condemned the radical adherents of the *koan* tradition for rejecting all the sutras and commentaries on the Buddha's doctrine, and for even challenging the authority of Bodhidharma. Emphasis on the present moment and assimilation to Taoist doctrine is all well and good. But the proponents of gradual enlightenment through *za-zen* could not accept their rivals' total rejection of history and tradition. These two streams of Chinese Zen flowed into Japan. In Japan, however, the opposition between them was not ideological but a matter of temperament and spiritual inclination. Men of brilliant wit and dynamic character would prefer the radical *koan* approach to instant enlightenment. Others, more subdued by nature, would choose the quiet deeds of everyday life and the peaceful sitting in *za-zen*. We'll take a closer look at these two schools of Zen as they existed in Japan. Dogen is the outstanding personage of the conservative *Soto* sect, and Hakuin is a great Master of the more radical *Rinzai* sect.

From the beginning of Japanese recorded history in the sixth century A.D. there is mention of intermittent visits by Chinese Zen monks to Japan. During these first centuries, however, it remained a Chinese import. Its influence was not strong. It was not until the thirteenth century that Zen took firm root in Japanese soil. For it was not until then that Japanese Masters arose who were capable of presenting Zen in ways suitable to Japanese culture. Among these original teachers, Zen Master Dogen (1200-1253) takes first place. He is venerated by all schools of Zen as a Bodhisattva, and he has been called in modern times the strongest and most original thinker that Japan has ever produced. He certainly is Japan's outstanding religious genius. We'll outline his life, his doctrine of *za-zen* and the philosophical underpinnings of this doctrine.

A sensitive child of noble birth, Dogen experienced early in life the transitoriness of all things when he was shocked at the age of two by the death of his father and at the age of seven by the loss of his mother. As she lay dying, his mother urged him to become a monk and work for the salvation of all sentient beings—the Bodhisattva ideal. Like Gautama Buddha he fled from his family and their desire to have him succeed in his aristocratic father's footsteps. Ordained a Buddhist monk at the age of thirteen he soon stumbled upon the question that was to occupy his life. The problem he brought to the older monks was this: If the primal Buddha-nature is already at the heart of every sentient being, then why all the effort and longing for enlightenment? In other words, if I am already the Buddha in my deepest reality, why strive to *become* a Buddha? Put another way, what is the difference between innate enlightenment and acquired enlightenment?

Not satisfied with the answers he received in Japan, Dogen was drawn to pursue his quest in China. He was finally directed to the experienced and famous Zen Master Ju-ching. The young monks meditated literally day and night under Ju-ching's kindly but uncompromising discipline. One day at night-time meditation Ju-ching noticed one of the disciples sleeping and he shouted, "In Zen, body and mind are cast off. Why do you sleep?" On hearing these words, Dogen was enlightened. Ju-ching confirmed Dogen's experience as authentic and approved him to succeed as a patriarch in the *Soto* sect. After further training in China, Dogen returned to Japan. Immediately he started writing his treatises on the practice of *za-zen* and in 1236 he founded the first fully independent Zen temple in Japan. There he guided his disciples, both men and women, in the single-minded pursuit of liberation. The precarious and transitory nature of human life overshadowed all his thoughts. In spite of change and death, this human life can be transfigured by the spirit, like the evaporating drop of dew reflects the light of the moon. This transfiguration is the one thing necessary. And until his death on August 28, 1253, Dogen's one compassionate concern was to show others the way to this enlightenment. *Za-zen* is the way. In *za-zen* is the realization of the whole of the Buddha's *dharma*. *Za-zen*, as we will see, was the answer to that one question which preoccupied his life, i.e., concerning the relationship of inborn enlightenment to acquired enlightenment.

Za-zen is meditation made sitting on a pillow, legs crossed Indian fashion in the Lotus position. Those who find this position too difficult can see Chapter I for alternative postures through which they can become at once relaxed and alert. Zen always adapts to the prevailing culture.[3] The point is enlightenment and not the mere imitation of the external trappings of a culture foreign to one's own. The body must be maintained upright. The light is to be subdued, neither too bright nor too dark. Eyes are open. Tongue is to be kept against the palate, lips and teeth closed. Thoughts and desires pass on the mental screen. Note them and dismiss them. Their feverish activity will gradually die down, concentration will come of its own accord, and the mind will be still like a tranquil lake.

In spite of the similarity of the sitting posture, *za-zen* is different in spirit from the *dhyana* of Indian Yoga. The contrast between Japanese Zen and Indian Yoga is brought out by their respective approaches to breathing in meditation. The Yogin seeks to control his breath, and practices formal exercises until he can breathe according to a pre-established rhythm. In *za-zen* there is a surrender to the spontaneous rhythm of the breathing process whose origin lies below all consciousness. Rather than consciously *breathing*, I let myself go so that I am *breathed* by my breath. When my breath is allowed to flow according to the utterly unique spontaneities of my own organism, it becomes an efficacious sign of contact with my own original nature, i.e., with my Buddha-nature.

Dogen saw a sacramental almost magical quality in this *za-zen* sitting breathing process itself. Body and mind are single unity. The man sitting quietly in tune with the spontaneous rhythms of his body is by that very fact in tune with the Way, the *tao*, his own Buddha-nature. And now for Dogen's greatest insight of all: The sitting-emptying spontaneous process of *za-zen* is not a *precondition* for enlightenment. *Za-zen* indeed in itself is *already* enlightenment! *Za-zen* is itself a revelation of the Buddha-nature, and so is an activity of incalculable worth. There is nothing I might better be doing than *za-zen*. This practice is the one thing necessary.

I miss the point entirely if I have the purpose of seeking Buddhahood by means of meditation. This blinds me to the fact that there is nothing to seek. My Buddha-nature is already there. This is *original* enlightenment. *Za-zen* is the revelation of this already present original nature. Such is *acquired* enlightenment. The focus is always on the present. I do not enter upon *za-zen* in expectation of a great experience. The present moment is the experience. In missing this, I miss everything. This is Dogen's solution to the riddle which plagued him from his youth. If I am already the Buddha, why do the great Masters instruct me to seek Buddhahood? *Za-zen* reveals to me the Buddha-nature that was there all along. Acquired enlightenment is based on original enlightenment. *Za-zen* is the simple direct and easy path.

Za-zen is demanding. Relentless practice is all that matters. But *za-zen* is uncomplicated. There are no great theories to master. Dogen's teaching, however, is firmly based on a profound metaphysical insight into reality. His simplified exclusive stress on *za-zen* rests on two metaphysical principles. First, *za-zen* is enlightenment. This we have already indicated. And second, the endless cycle of Becoming (*samsara*) is identical with the perfect rest of *nirvana*.

First, the identity of *za-zen* and enlightenment rests on the doctrine of the inborn Buddha-nature of all sentient beings. I need not look outside myself for my true reality. It is already present within. The seed is there. This is primal or original enlightenment. But without the practice of *za-zen*, my Buddha-nature does not manifest itself. The self-revelation of my original nature is acquired enlightenment. It comes not *by means of* the practice of *za-zen*. Rather, *za-zen is* this acquired enlightenment. Za-zen *is* the manifestation of my original nature.

The Buddha-nature is not hidden in all things. Rather all things exactly as they appear are the Buddha. The Buddha does not lie behind appearances. Rather, the appearances are the Buddha. There is no need of endless stages on the way to salvation. All that is needed is *za-zen*. And *za-zen* simply takes note of what is already present. There is no distinction between means and end, hope and fulfillment, desire and object. *Za-zen* is a way of unity of body and mind. *Za-zen* is a way of unity with Nature and all beings. It is not an extraordinary experience unless I want to say that the very ordinary is extraordinary.

Dogen's second metaphysical principle is that *samsara*, the cycle of becoming, is identical with *nirvana*, perfect rest. In the present, time stands still. Every instant is self-contained. As we saw in Jung's synchronous view of the universe, the All is contained in the individual and the individual comprises the All. The present moment does not look toward future fulfillment. Rather the *now* is sufficient unto itself. Every moment of *za-zen* is of infinite worth because every moment contains all that there is. The whole of my fleeting life is realized in each present moment. The flux of Becoming when actualized in the present instant becomes perfect rest. In this way, *za-zen* tempers the sad realization of the transitoriness of human life. In *za-zen* each fleeting instant is perceived as an eternal fullness. Self-actualization for Dogen is not that assertive search for individual fulfillment which characterizes modern psychology. The keynote, rather, is reverence for the Buddha-nature in oneself and all things. The way to know oneself is self-surrender, and the self-surrender of *za-zen* is itself the enlightened experience of all things.

Actually, Dogen's contemporary, Eisai, is named as the founder of Japanese Zen. A member of the *Rinzai* sect, he taught the doctrine of sudden enlightenment and the use of the *koan*. We'll look at *Rinzai* Zen, however, through the eyes of its modern reformer, Hakuin (1685-1768). Hakuin is responsible for the development of Zen in modern Japan, and is honored as the greatest of Zen Masters, next to Dogen. His temperament was passionate and sensitive. His life story is a series of profound psychological and religious crises dating from early boyhood to the end of his life. His path to enlightenment was not characterized by the quiet rhythms of *za-zen*. Rather, his Way was a continual fierce life-and-death wrestling with the riddle of human existence presented by the *koan*. Where *Soto* Zen points to a path of slow steady progress, the rhythm of *Rinzai* Zen is a leap from a state of deep despair and shattering doubt to a glorious and equally shattering enlightenment. The greater the doubt, the greater is the force of the resulting enlightenment. *Rinzai* Zen, to borrow the words of Jesus, brings not peace, but the sword. It comes to cast fire upon the earth. And that sword and that fire come in the shape of the *koan*.

A *koan* (two-syllable word) is an anecdote, statement, question, or riddle posed by an ancient Master and devised to open up the mind to the truth of Zen. Its intent is shock-value, i.e., to cause doubt, consternation, frustration, bewilderment. In a word, the *koan* is designed to jolt the mind out of its rational complacent ordinary way of looking at things in order to provoke the transformation of consciousness which is Zen enlightenment. The *koan* is not enlightenment. It is an instrument or device for producing enlightenment.

One of the most famous *koan* was invented by Hakuin when he was an old man. "Clap your hands," he would tell his disciples, "and you hear a sound. Now tell me, what is the sound of a single hand?" The *koan* is not a child's riddle or a witty joke. The Master demands that the disciple devote his whole mind and energy to wrestling with the problem. The *koan* is meant to "hook" the disciple into an inquiry that will absorb his whole life and, if successful, will lead to enlightenment. The Master is the sole arbiter of the "correct solution," of authentic enlightenment. The disciple wrestles with the *koan* day and night for months and even years.

The *koan* of the sound of one hand could be approached intellectually. I might say, for example, that the sound of two hands clapping is part of the ordinary world of Becoming (*samsara*). But the sound of one hand is not like any ordinary sound. It transcends all

sound. The sound of one hand is a symbol of the unconditioned principle of the universe where all distinctions
disappear. I might continue to explain that my one
hand exists in this ordinary world, but that it simulta-
neously points to the unconditioned world (*nirvana*). I
could then conclude that the proper solution to the
koan is the understanding that *samsara* and *nirvana* are
one. Were I to present such a rational intellectual explanation of the *koan* to my Master, he would most
likely hit me on the head with a bamboo pole. Zen is
not rationality and metaphysics. A good knock on the
head would at least bring me back to the realm of experience!

The *koan* has a very precise objective. It is meant to
arouse in me a state of doubt, and to push that doubt to
its furthest limits. The Master will reject every rational
answer I bring to him and will send me back to continue looking for an answer. The double bind, the frustration, the doubt become unbearable. No answer is ac-
ceptable and yet an answer must be found. The disciple
goes to Hakuin with his solutions, and Hakuin shakes
his head and again raises his one hand. Logic breaks
and shatters against that immovable wall, the sight of
Hakuin's upraised hand. There is no way around it and
yet a way must be found.

Well, what *is* the sound of one hand clapping? Any
conceptualized verbalized answer is automatically
wrong. A sound is not the word "sound." A hand is
not the word "hand." The Zen Master is not practicing
a *koan* "system" on his disciples. Zen is simple absolute experience. The Zen Master does not talk about
enlightenment, but he *acts* from the fullness of his enlightened experience. The fullness of Zen experience

baffles every attempt at rationality. As the Zen saying goes:

"Before I studied Zen, mountains were mountains, rivers were rivers, and valleys were valleys. [I knew the meaning of two hands clapping.]

"While I was studying Zen, mountains were no longer mountains, rivers no longer rivers, and valleys were no longer valleys. [What is the sound of one hand? —rationality thwarted the extremity of doubt ensues.]

"After I was enlightened, mountains were mountains again, rivers were rivers, and valleys were valleys. [Concrete experience is not esoteric, and neither is Zen nor the sound of one hand clapping.]"

The Way of Zen is a Way that leaves all ways. It's so simple and direct as to be ineffable. Rather than a way, it's more like getting lost. You'll see more of the woods, won't you, if you wander around "lost" than if you stick to the beaten track?

Consider some of the replies given to the question, "What is Zen ultimately?"

"Willows are green and flowers are pink."
"A short person is short; a tall person is tall."
"The moon is in the sky; water is in the jar."
"Every day is a good day."[4]

To get back to Hakuin, what occasioned his enlightenment? He was studying the Buddhist *Sutras* one day when the humming of a bee aroused him from his concentration. With a start, he cried out and wept. Immediately he directly and simply saw through to the heart of all things. Such is Zen, profound in its simplicity. As we quoted in Chapter I:

Sitting quietly doing nothing,
Spring comes, and the grass grows by itself.

The *za-zen* of the *Soto* sect and the *koan* exercises of
Rinzai Zen both had their origins in China. In China
these methods were opposed to one another, but the
Japanese saw them as complementary and often practiced them together. Such was the Japanese way. More
characteristic, still, of Japanese Zen was the way that
Zen found expression in the arts. Painting, archery,
flower arranging, ceremonial tea, gardening, and poetry
all had a peculiar Zen flavor. We'll illustrate the artistic
turn in Zen by a look at Japan's greatest poet, Matsuo
Basho (1644-1694).

Basho's poetic genius is appreciated even in the West
for his perfecting of the exquisite *haiku* form of verse.
Basho was not a monk, but he was a lay follower of
Zen. His poetry is filled with the simple straightforward
innocence of Zen experience, the Zen love of nature,
and the Buddha's Middle Way. His poems set the stan-
dards of *haiku* verse which are used to the present day.
Basho felt that artistic attunement with nature is precisely the spirit that permeates the best of Japanese
painting, the rhythms of Japanese song, and the rituals
of the tea ceremony. In following nature his poetry
creatively transforms life. His thoughts are of the
moon. He beholds the form of the flower in everything
he sees. He is a friend of the seasons, and in their successive rhythms he learns the rhythms of human living.
Zen is best expressed through poetry and art, not
through philosophy, since Zen is a matter of experience
rather than of thought.

Haiku is a spare, epigrammatic, stripped-down verse
form only seventeen syllables long. There are five sylla-

bles in the first line, then seven, then five in the third
line. This extreme economy of expression forces the
poet to say much in a little space. He has seventeen syllables in which to both evoke a mood and paint a picture which stirs the imagination. The *haiku* is demanding on the reader, too. The artist provides the spark.
The reader must enter in and be kindled. The *haiku* is
like a high-speed camera catching life in the instant, in
the here and now as it flows. Usually, too, the *haiku*
has a reference to a particular season of year. The
changing seasons are one experience we all have in
common. But *haiku* is not to be dismissed as mere "nature poetry." Crucial is the human feeling evoked by
nature and the seasons. *Haiku*, then, becomes an expression and an instrument of Zen mysticism.

Listen to Basho as he mourns the death of his young
friend, the poet Issho:

Grave, bestir thyself!
My mournful voice weeps
Like the autumn wind.[5]

The dying glow of autumn, the chill winds, the dead
young man, and Basho's sorrow all fuse in one exquisite image. This sorrow is not despair. The changing
seasons teach that death is part of life.

Though Basho was not a monk, he was an enlightened disciple of Zen. His heart was empty of desire. He
carried the word within him. His was the lonely profound inner quiet of the mystic. That absolute silence
he found one day in nature, and expressed it in a beautiful *haiku* poem. The spot was a mountain temple built
on rock. Not a soul was stirring. In grand stillness the
temple was perched high above the everyday human

bustle. Basho writes of this encounter with perfect quiet:

> Only silence alone—
> Into the rocky cliff penetrates
> The sound of the cicada.[6]

How deafening can be the chirp of a cricket or the croak of a frog in the dead stillness of night. The high-pitched drone of the cicada, for Basho, accents the utter and absolute tranquillity of nature—and of the enlightened heart.

When one is in touch with one's original nature, one sees Nature with one's original eyes. The naked innocent experience is all:

> The old pond.
> A frog jumps in.
> Plop![7]

The Zen adept is born again. The natural child inside, killed by civilization, rationality, passions, and conventions, is reborn. Consider a little boy walking happily through the woods, listening to the chirping, warbling, squawking and cooing of the birds. The boy's father with the best of intentions seizes this opportunity to "broaden" his son's experience. "That," he tells the boy, "is a woodpecker. Over there is a sparrow." Immediately for the lad the delightful flow of birdsong dries up. Now he is concerned with which is the sparrow and which the woodpecker. Experience has not been broadened but narrowed. Anxiety and rationality replace delight and intuition. *Haiku* is an invitation to return to the freedom and directness of my Buddha-nature:

Simply trust:
Do not the petals flutter down
Just like that?[8]

The western delusion consists in thinking that if only I be rational enough all problems will be solved. The Zen approach says, Stop being rational and all problems will dissolve.

Zen, especially in its *Rinzai* and its artistic forms, is less concerned with an Absolute or a God than any other mystical tradition. There is little or no mention of philosophical or religious ideas like *Brahman, nirvana* and *tao*. The "ism" has been dropped from Chinese naturalism. Nature-Experience-Now: That's all there is because that's everything there is. Flower-arranging, architecture, ceremonial tea, and poetry all express this simple insight. But Zen is not an esoteric preserve for artists. For the Zennist, everyday life with its ordinary activities becomes a work of art. "When eating, just eat; when sleeping, just sleep; when walking, just walk. And above all, don't wobble!" The great Zen Master Dogen received his first deep impression of Zen from a temple cook who had come into town to do the shopping. The cook would not take time to discuss Zen with the young seeker. He had to return to the monastery where his daily round of activities in the kitchen was the practice of enlightenment. Ask such a monk the secret of Zen and he'll tell you to wash the dishes. Although we have outlined above that philosophy which underlies the practice and experience of Zen, it is doubtful that a Zen monastery would support a resident philosopher or theologian! Philosophy and theology move us away from the total organism to the mind, and away from the present to the abstract and timeless.

How few of us live in the place and time where we are.
"When sleeping, just sleep," says Zen. But I toss and
turn, concerned about the morrow. "When eating, just
eat." But filled with regret at the morning's failure, I
lunch without tasting the food at all. This experiential
non-doctrinal side of Zen stressed by Suzuki and Watts
has made it most adaptable to the western world. No
new doctrines to learn. Zen points the way to concrete
experience which transcends all cultures. We have seen
how the whole story is not so simple. Zen, like every
other way of life, has a history and a cultural form.

The vigor, subtlety, and peculiar Japanese character
of Zen was not lost on the first Europeans ever to encounter it in the middle of the sixteenth century. It was
then that Christian evangelists, mostly Spanish, first
touched the shores of Japan. Even in that far from ecumenical age, these missionaries acknowledged the wit
and virtue of the Zen Masters they encountered. Zen
Buddhism was the religion they felt presented them
with their greatest challenge. Jesuit missionary Francis
Xavier considered the Japanese the most superior and
intelligent people he had discovered. They asked questions, he felt, that neither Thomas Aquinas nor Duns
Scotus had foreseen. Their asceticism and intellectual-
ism he admired. Their doctrines (reincarnation and implied pantheism) he abominated. Their mysticism he
seems not to have understood or realized. Persecution, of
course, was provoked by Xavier's condemnation of Zen
doctrine as the work of the devil. It says a lot for the
tolerance and open-mindedness of the mystical Zen
spirit that so many monks befriended these fiery Spanish missionaries, engaged them in lengthy religious dis-
putations, and even converted to Christianity! For example, one octogenarian monk at Daito Kuji, curious

about the strange beliefs of Europeans and Indians, listened to a Father Vilela. Such was his amazement and admiration of Christian doctrine that he agreed to be baptized, receiving, of course, a good Christian name, Fabiao Meison. A more sensational event was the conversion of Kesshu, a Zen Master whose enlightenment had been twice confirmed. Are such unlikely events due to the persistence of the missionaries, or to the Zen mystic's unconcern with confessional forms, or to an inherent human void at the heart of Zen? This author remains completely baffled. Today the situation is reversed. Attracted to the very mysticism that the sixteenth-century missionaries were unable to recognize, many people in the western world are looking to Zen for freedom, spontaneity, and liberation from what they feel is the rigid tyranny of Christianity.

In conclusion, Zen recapitulates in itself all the various oriental interpretations of mystical experience that we have encountered. India is represented in the mysterious figure of Bodhidharma, who brought Buddhism into China. Bodhidharma assured Zen of an authentic link with original Buddhism, and at the same time he underlined two features that were to particularly characterize the practice of Zen, namely, *za-zen* or sitting meditation and instantaneous enlightenment. In China, Buddhism adapted to the Taoist spirit. It became more concrete and practical, and less theoretical. It became more this-worldly and less other-worldly, and more concerned with Nature and less focused on psychology. Two traditions of Zen developed in the forms of the *Lin-chi* sect which became *Rinzai* Zen in Japan and of the *Ts'ao-tung* sect which became *Soto* Zen in Japan. The former was more plebian and dynamic. It stressed the use of the *koan* as a means to instantaneous enlightenment. The latter was more passive and monkish. It saw the practice of *za-zen* as itself a gradually developing enlightenment. *Rinzai* disciples accused *Soto* Zen of inertia. *Za-zen* or "just sitting," they felt, enervates the mind. *Soto* disciples in turn pointed to the dangers of the *koan* exercises. The deliberate irrationality of *Rinzai* Zen increases the possibility of self-delusion. An individual is worse off for putting himself beyond all theories and all morality in the name of an enlightenment that is not authentic or is only partial.

In Japan the opposition between these two sects became less severe. *Rinzai* Masters kept their disciples well in line and disciplined in their practice of the *koan*. And *za-zen* in *Soto* monasteries was an intensely active type of concentration. Temperament rather than dogma came to govern the path one chose. Dogen, the greatest name in Japanese Zen, abhorred all sectarian divisiveness. Contemplative in spirit, he recommended *za-zen* as the sure and easy practice of enlightenment for all. Hakuin, on the other hand, the great *Rinzai* reformer, was by temperament intensely sensitive and hyperactive. His life is the story of one long wrestling bout with the *koan*, until at the very end he might have said:

> Sick from the journey;
> Chasing on the dry field
>   Dreams go round.[9]

Such are the words of the final *haiku* to flow from the brush of Japan's greatest poet, Basho.

Like Zen in China and Japan, Zen in the West is founded on the acceptance of one's own Buddha-nature.

You don't have to go to Japan to discover your original face. As Dogen told his disciples, you will never find the truth in foreign lands if you cannot find it in your own sitting place where you are now.

KABALAH—JEWISH MYSTICISM. RABBI DR. JOSEPH GELBER-MAN, HASSIDIC MASTER, LEADING A KABALISTIC MEDI-

IX
Mysticism or Masochism?

Our survey of the great oriental traditions certainly shows mysticism to be congenial to eastern ways of thinking and practical for eastern ways of living. The western world in the personages of people like Plotinus, Meister Eckhardt, and John of the Cross is not without its own mystical tradition. But Christianity, Judaism, and Mohammedanism, as prophetic religions, have never made mysticism central and essential to salvation. In fact, more often the mystic is held suspect. In the name of his own private illuminations he is liable to ignore or minimize the teaching of the prophets. Also, he is liable to bypass prophetic meditation in an effort at direct union with the divine.

There are more serious charges against mysticism than its alleged incompatibility with prophetic religion. Sociologist Peter Berger sees the practice of mysticism as basically masochistic.[1] The self-denial, the withdrawal and the disappearance of the individual are all anti-human. Mysticism is a refusal to affirm and develop the self. It is not a means of self-realization but a pathology. From another point of view, the work of anthropologist Mary Douglas lends support to a similar objection.[2] Mysticism, she says, tends to be cultivated by groups who exist at the fringes of society, i.e., groups which are not in the mainstream. Ecstasy, trance, and mystical prayer are much more likely to flourish among hippies, nuns, and racial minorities,

whereas the same trance-like behavior would be
frowned on at the Chamber of Commerce or in the
WASP cathedral in the suburbs. In other words, mysticism is a symptom of social alienation. All is not well
with the social life of the mystic. Barred from the world
of human affairs, he takes refuge in the divine. Again,
mysticism is a sign not of human fulfillment but of
human alienation.

To sum up, then, we have noted three basic objections against mysticism as a human ideal. First, the
mystic claims to see through social conventions and
rules. His enlightenment places him above ordinary
morality. The mystic is not trustworthy enough to be a
"company man." This first objection comes from the
well-organized and dogmatic prophetic religions. The
mystic is not without honor, but he is suspect as a potential rebel. He seems not to take the official game
seriously enough. Sociologist Peter Berger proposes a
second objection which is just the opposite. Mystical
prayer involved an emptying out of self in order to sub-
mit to God and religion. The character of the mystic is
basically masochistic. He practices self-denial in order
to be dominated by powers that lie outside himself.
Mysticism is not a way of self-realization but of self-
destruction. The mystic is not the potential rebel
against religion but the perfect *subject*, i.e., he subjects
himself to religion to the point of self-annihilation.
Third, anthropologist Mary Douglas highlights the social impotence of the mystic. The mystic, she points
out, exists at the fringes of established society. Removed from the effective centers of human power, his
refuge is to seek powers beyond the human. We end up
with three separate but related "put-downs" of mysticism as a valid human ideal. The mystic is a potential

rebel (objection one). The mystic is masochistic (objection two). The mystic is a social outcast (objection three).

Psychiatrist Thomas Harris (*I'm OK—You're OK*) has made a remarkably fresh analysis of the psychology of mystical experience.[3] His psychological method is the approach called Transactional Analysis. The resulting framework enables us to sort out these various ambivalent and negative assessments of mystical experience. Surely I do not want to undertake the mystical quest if it is anti-human and destructive. Which is mysticism, a path toward self-realization or toward self-impoverishment? It could be either, says Harris. *Self* is the crucial word that needs analysis. So first we will outline the components of the self. Then we will see how this analysis enables us to distinguish two kinds of mysticism, one healthy and fulfilling, the other sick and regressive. Finally, with this tool in hand, we will take a closer look at the three objections against mysticism and try to evaluate them in the light of Harris' analysis.

The mystic speaks over and over again of loss of self. The negative way of meditation involves the overcoming of self. *Sankhya-yoga* prescribes a way of letting go of ego. Buddhism preaches the doctrine of *anatta* (No-Self). In Taoism, my *te* or power is the power of the cosmic *tao*. The mystics speak also of finding the self. For the Vedantin, this is the realization that *Atman* is *Brahman*. For the Buddhist, it is the discovery of one's Buddha-nature. Taoist mysticism is rewarded by a glimpse of *p'u*, one's original nature. What is this self that is lost? What is this self that is found?

The hypothesis of Transactional Analysis is that there is not one self, but three. I carry around with me three selves, a little Child, a Parent, and an Adult. The actions of the little Child in me are controlled by feelings and feelings alone. The Parent in me speaks and behaves dogmatically, authoritatively and self-righteously. The grown-up Adult in me is reasonable, logical, and responsible. This is not mere theory. My Child is actually observable to others, and to myself if I'm honest and aware enough. And the same goes for my Parent and my Adult. I go through the day shifting gears. Sometimes my Child is in charge, sometimes my Parent, and other times the Adult in me.

Not surprisingly, the Parent in me was put there by my parents during the first few years of my life. Utterly helpless, I was completely dependent on them for survival, for information and for values. Everything they did and said got burned into my mind and blood. "God sees everything you do." "Don't talk to strangers." "Never trust a Jew." "Better safe than sorry." "Children should be seen and not heard." "Elbows off the table when you eat." "Turn the mattress every day." "Close your mouth when you chew." "A black cat means bad luck." "The devil is waiting to take your soul to hell." "Drink will ruin your life." "Mother knows best." "A mortal sin makes your soul turn black." "Stay away from the stove." "Don't cross in the middle of the street." "Cover your mouth when you sneeze." "Always dry the silverware first."

Clearly much of this data of my Parent was useful and even necessary to my survival as a child. Whether or not I understood the reasons, it was to my advantage to avoid jay-walking or being too friendly with strangers. Some was false and harmful: "Never trust a Jew." And some was ambiguous as when my father said, "Always speak out what's on your mind," and my mother countered with, "Children should be seen and not heard." But all these data, whether useful, harmful, or conflicting, were uncritically accepted and precisely recorded without modification in the Parent self formed in my early childhood and carried with me throughout life. When my parents took me out to a restaurant, I would spot a child at a nearby table and say to my mother, "Look at that bad boy; he has his elbows on the table." This was my Parent speaking. And when today with children of my own, I clear my throat and say quite pompously, "Take your elbows off the table when you eat," this is the exact same Parent speaking.

There is a second self in me formed during my earliest years and carried with me the rest of my life. This is the little Child that responded to the Parent. It is a faithful tape-recording of all the reactions and feelings of the helpless little Child toward his super all-knowing Parents. Confronted with the daily barrage of commands, caveats, prohibitions, condemnations, it's no surprise that the basic feeling the Child comes to live with is "I'm no good, failed again, my fault, can never do anything right." On the one hand, my Child has inborn urges to create, to be curious, to explore, to learn, to experience, and on the other hand he has these constant uncompromising demands from the Parent to stifle curiosity, to watch his step, to turn off creativity if he wants to get the approval of his parents or of God, the super-Parent. In other words, to use Harris' language, the inborn "OK feelings" get smothered under a mountain of "not OK feelings."

These precise feelings precisely as recorded I carry about with me throughout my lifetime. In other words, no matter how grown-up I may appear on the outside, on the inside my Child is always there in the wings ready to take over. If my boss looks at me crooked, I feel guilty and depressed even though I'm not conscious of having done anything wrong. That's my not-OK Child reacting. I'm with a group discussing politics. I don't speak up, but say to myself, "Who'd want to hear my opinion." ("Children should be seen and not heard.") But sometimes the curious, creative, playful OK-Child breaks through. And I come up to my wife who is over the stove, give her a kiss and dance her around the room. Or I take an afternoon off to tinker and fool with my hi-fi set. Or I play the happy Irishman on St. Patrick's Day at the office. This Child with its reservoir of taped OK and not-OK feelings is the second self which is part of my permanent identity. The third self is the Adult.

The Adult is the self in me that is guided by my own thinking, testing and experimenting. The little boy reaches for the knob on the TV set. "Don't touch that!" his mother shouts. He pulls back, but you can be sure that the first chance he gets he's going to see what that knob is all about. That's his Adult self getting born in him. My Adult processes the dogmatic tapes of the Parent so I can find out for myself if they are really true. My Adult examines my Child's feeling processes to learn if they are really appropriate. At a party in fear I avoid a stranger. My Adult asks, "Is this fear a suitable reaction? Or is it my Child's automatic response to my Parent's dogmatic 'Never talk to strangers'?" My Parent and my Child are both still very much with me. But if my Adult is in control, my Adult decides whether these tapes should be played. My Adult can decide that "Be careful crossing the street" is a useful automatic Parental rule to follow, while "Never talk to strangers" is a rule to be suppressed as archaic and unsuitable. My Adult can decide that my Child's delight in making puns is a help in my social life, but my automatic fear of policemen is my automatic Child's reaction to authority now outmoded.

The strong Adult self has his Parent and his Child under good control and is free for his main job which is to estimate rationally the probable consequences of various decisions. The Adult, once it is free from checking out the Parent and Child and free too from being dominated by them, is open for new business. The natural curiosity and creativity of the Child is harnessed and directed by the Adult. The result is an integrated, self-actualizing, creative human being. We will use this analysis of the Parent-Adult-Child selves to help us understand and meet objections brought against mystical experience by the sociologist and anthropologist. First, what is to be said about sociologist Peter Berger's charge that the practice of mysticism is essentially masochistic?

The masochistic attitude is essentially self-destructive rather than self-assertive. Is the self-emptying process of mysticism (e.g., the Negative Way) a type of psychological suicide? How does Berger arrive at such a jaundiced view of mysticism?

His analysis of mysticism is bound up with his analysis of religion and how it functions in society. As a sociologist he asks: What is religion supposed to do for a society? Religion is as religion does. Mysticism is as mysticism does. The function of religion, says Berger, is to bring order and meaning into the chaos of human experience. "The chaos of human experience"—isn't this an exaggerated expression? Is a world without God or religion really a world without sense or meaning? It is true that in the modern day especially the greater part of our lives can make perfect sense without religion.

The bulk of our lives is taken up with ordinary everyday activities in a world whose meaning and reality are taken for granted. If we have any questions, we're more likely to ask the psychologist, the nutritionist, the politician, or the lawyer for answers rather than the priest or minister. As a matter of fact, precisely for this reason, many clergymen feel like they have become redundant, superfluous. Seminaries are likely to have more courses in group dynamics, counseling, psychology and management than they have in theology. Clergymen are more likely to be found at a political demonstration or psychological encounter session than they are in the church or the meditation room. Rather than functioning as guru, the modern clergyman is more likely to be block parent, social organizer, and marriage counselor. One might say that they have sold out to the modern myth that science is sufficiently able to make sense out of our lives and give them meaning. Unfortunately this is not the case. And it is precisely where science falls short that religion comes into play.

There is a dimension of human life that escapes scientific planning and control. There are certain kinds of events that rudely shatter the routines of daily living. There are certain problems that all the science and all the rational planning in the world cannot begin to cope with. That which human effort can cope with and control we'll call natural. That which escapes human efforts and control we'll call supernatural. The supernatural is the province of religion and mysticism. What are these supernatural events?

Death, chronic illness, accidents, suffering, failures, frustrations are all an inevitable part of being human. Reason and planning cannot eliminate them from our lives, yet somehow we must cope with them. Hope, creativity, wonder, love as well as despair, boredom, and hatred are also inextricably bound up with being human. Again, reason and planning cannot tell me why I should hope rather than despair or forgive rather than hate. Indeed, science can't tell me why I should even bother to do science, use my reason, or make plans at all. Yet, if I am to go on living, I need a reason and meaning for living. Complacency in my daily routines carries me just so far. The death of a loved one or the anticipation of my own death calls all these into question. Or in the midst of a cheerfully successful life I am struck down with illness or a disabling accident. My life is turned upside down. What made sense before now becomes senseless overnight. The reality and meaning of my life is a frail and precarious thing indeed. I live at the edge of chaos. I'm always a heartbeat away from death. Where do I get the reasons that reason cannot give me? It is the function of religion, says Berger, to bring order and meaning into the chaos of human experience.

This religious meaning comes at a price. It demands submission to an Order and Reality that is greater than the human, greater than myself. It requires an emptying out of self so that I may be filled with the Divine, the Cosmic, the Universal Reality. Mysticism, says Berger, is the expression *par excellence* of this attitude. How does the mystic grow as a human being? He must first deny his own unique human individual ego. This human ego does not represent the law of his growth. Rather it represents illusion. God must increase. I must decrease. For the merely human laws of development, I must substitute the divine law within. At its deepest level human reality is not human at all, but divine. In this way, the mystic transcends the world of the human.

It is no longer Jack Jones that lives, but Christ speaking and acting through him. In the same way the devout Chinese peasant is guided not by his merely human energies, but by the law of the *tao* itself which is the universal rhythm of all things. The Hindu lives by Brahman and the Buddhist ego dissolves into *nirvana*. Microcosm dissolves into macrocosms. Unique authentic individuality disappears into the Absolute like a snowflake melting into the ocean of divinity.

Death, suffering, failure, frustration all defied my rational control. For the mystic, these problems are not rationally solved, but are transrationally *dis*-solved. What matters individual human death and suffering if I am united to Eternal Life and Divine Bliss? Suffering and death belong to the realm of *samsara, maya,* illusion. This realm is trivial compared to the overwhelming experience of the realm of the divine. Such, says Berger, is the mystic's masochistic solution to the insoluble problems of human living. Masochism is psychological self-annihilation. It is the turning in against the self of destructive tendencies. So the mystic systematically sets out to destroy his unique individual human reality. His senses are disciplined and withdrawn from their natural objects. His phantasies and feelings are stilled. Then his very ideas and mind become empty. Finally he loses even the sense of his own ego. The annihilation is complete. The masochism is perfect. This ideal is epitomized both in the Hebraeo-Christian canonization of the suffering Job submitting to complete destruction by the biblical God and in the *Ch'an* Buddhist story of Bodhidharma who sat for nine years facing a wall until his legs withered away.

If Berger is right, mysticism is *not* a valid human ideal. In fact, nothing could be more anti-human than the practice of mysticism. It provides a path not to self-discovery and fulfillment, but to self-annihilation. What is this *self* that would be annihilated? "Self," as we saw at the beginning of the chapter, is an ambiguous word. Transactional Analysis shows that we carry about with us not one Self, but three, a Parent, an Adult, and a Child. In this framework, how do we describe Berger's view of mystical experience? The mystics, Berger seems to say, have a Child-Parent relationship with the Divine. The Child in the mystic completely surrenders to the Parent. More than this, mystical experience is a complete sell-out to God, the super-Parent. By this complete acceptance of Divine Parental Authority, the Child becomes omnipotent. The Child acts, yes, but no longer the Child, for the power of the super-Parent acts through the Child. In total conformity and surrender, the Child sees in the super-Parent his real Self. This omnipotence comes at a price. The cost is high—no less than the annihilation of the Adult. The rational, responsible, independent Adult Self must die. The reward for this self-surrender of the Adult is the ecstasy of living by the power of the omnipotent super-Parent, and the joy and security of complete union with this Parent.

If this is the psychological shape of my practice of mysticism, then clearly I am on a path of neurosis and self-destruction (destruction of the Adult, that is). This is why it is important to have a trusted guru who will take me in hand if he sees I am taking this neurotic path. The mystical quest is too dangerous to undertake alone. It can so easily become a pseudo-mystical way of escaping from reality rather than a genuine experiential discovery of reality. If it results in the Adult dying so that the super-Parent may reign Supreme, then what passes for mysticism is counterfeit and anti-human. We would contend that the experience of genuine mystics is not masochistic, does not involve the death of the Adult self, and is a valid human ideal. We will point out how genuine mysticism differs from the counterfeit variety after considering a second objection against mysticism, that suggested by anthropologist Mary Douglas.

For Douglas, mysticism is a symptom of social pathology and human alienation. Not only is the mystic a neurotic as Berger contends, but he is a social misfit, or more precisely, a social drop-out. Her anthropological studies have led Douglas to distinguish four types of societies, ranging from those that are highly organized and demand intense loyalty to those that are vague, amorphous, and unstructured. It is in the latter that she finds mysticism and trance-like behavior flourishing. A complex and self-involving social structure is unfavorable to mysticism. Absence of clearly defined group boundaries and clearly defined roles results in an environment that fosters the practice of mysticism. Let's look at the three social climates unsuitable for mysticism so that we can contrast them with the climate in which mystics feel most at home.

There are societies where the stress is on loyalty and on the importance of belonging. The group is everything. The individual is nothing without the group. I think here of the Greek City-State where civil disobedience was unthinkable, where exile was worse than capital punishment. The exile belonged to the realm of the living dead. Without a society to call his own, his individual existence had no meaning anymore. I think of the medieval Roman Church where excommunication was the direst of penalties and the excommunicate belonged no longer to the society of heaven or that of earth. Or I think of a society like seventeenth-century

England where ostracism was a punishment worse than death. To be "sent to Coventry" was to be destroyed as an individual. In such societies where the group is all that matters, passive conformity is the cardinal virtue. Disloyalty is the capital sin. Fixed, formal, socially defined rituals make up the practice of religion. Nothing so individualistic as mysticism would be encouraged.

Second, there are societies where the emphasis is switched from the group to the individual. Belonging to a particular group is not important, but the expectations and roles demanded of a particular individual are all important. The post-technological society of the modern western world is the primary example. Tight loyal affiliation to groups is minimal. Outside the parents-children unit, family ties are loose. Church affiliations are more fluid. Mixed marriages and cross-denominational worship become as much the rule as the exception. There is little strong loyalty to the company one works for. Job mobility becomes the standard practice and ideal. One is expected to "hang loose" with regard to groups so that he can develop himself and advance as an individual. Many varied and complex demands, however, are placed upon the individual. He is expected to complete long years of education, to get a good job and to move up the ladder continually. He is expected to acquire a car and a color TV set and an endlessly expanding list of consumer goods from electric carving knives to hygiene deodorants. His is the burden to provide all these and more for his wife and his children. Individual achievement and success is the cardinal virtue of such a society. Such a social setting does not, according to Douglas, encourage mysticism. Rather, religion in America, for example, is mainly ethical in emphasis. It focuses on individual achievement, hard work, and doing good for others. Mystical detachment from material things and withdrawal from others would be deviant behavior indeed in a society like ours.

The third type of society unfavorable to mystics combines the qualities of the first two. On the one hand, the group is important. Belonging is essential. Everyone knows and cares who is in and who is out. On the other hand, the roles and expectations of the individual are also highly organized and structured. I think of a society like Vatican City. The group is Roman Catholic and it is important to belong. And individuals within the group have carefully defined roles. Each caste— Pope, Cardinal, Bishop, Priest, Layman—has its privileges and duties. And within each caste the hierarchical pecking order is understood by all. Armies, prisons, monasteries, and mental hospitals manifest a similar social structure. It is in this third type of society that behavior is most tightly controlled. Group definition and individual role assignment both combine to structure the activity of the members. The cardinal virtue in such a society is the fulfillment of one's prescribed duty in and to the group. Neglect of the group, "goofing off," is the capital sin. The group demands that the members show loyalty by playing their respective parts in the successful functioning of the whole. Duty and ritual are the prime expressions of religion. Identity comes from the outside, not from a mystical inner quest.

Where in the world do we locate the mystic? In what social setting does he belong? It is the claim of Mary Douglas that the structured behavior of the above types of society is inimical to mysticism. As social control is strengthened, one becomes deaf to the inner voice.

There is a fourth type of society where structure and controls are at a minimum. Here's where the mystic flourishes. First, from the side of the group, "belonging" is unimportant in this fourth kind of society. No one cares who is in and who is out. There are no formal requirements for membership. Second, there are little or no expectations placed upon the individual. He is free to evolve, develop and act anyway he wishes, to find and do "his own thing." I think of the anchorites and hermits sequestered in the desert in the early Christian Church. I think of open-house communes and pads where "hippies" float in and out, or of the pygmy tribes that wander loosely through the African forests. The cardinal virtues are sincerity, authenticity, and fidelity to oneself. Capital sins are those against the self: hypocrisy, cruelty, and submitting to frustration. The mood is romantic. The individual escapes from the toils of social control to find his own authentic rhythms. Religion is spontaneous and unritualistic. There is no commitment to fellow human beings to work together in achieving common goals or building up society. Looks, or touches, or inarticulate grunts can suffice for communication. Others are suffused in a benign ineffectual good will. The individual's communion with himself, with nature, or with God takes primacy over all external relationships. In a word, anthropologist Mary Douglas views the mystic as a social *drop-out*. Mysticism is a path of withdrawal and escape for the alienated in society, that is, for those who are unable to create and sustain strong social relationships. They withdraw to the fringes of that established society with which they cannot cope. And there at the fringe, liberated from those social controls they found so impossible and frustrating, they are free to pursue their own path in benign loneliness.

What is the psychological structure of Mary Douglas' alienated mystic, the social drop-out? His character remains blurred, vague, and undefined both from the side of society (social controls) and from the side of the individual (role and goal expectations to be fulfilled). At the fringes of society where this mystic lives, the authoritarian dogmatic Parent is dead. There is no code of the group to conform to, no criterion of belonging, no membership fees, no baptism or rite of passage. Indeed this liberation from the Parent is not a rebirth, a passage to a new level, say, of Adult being. The Parent self has not died in order that the Adult might live. No. Rather, the psychological refrain is, "The Parent is dead, long live the Child!" For, among other examples, these are the flower children. They have all the graces and foibles that make the Child at once such a wonderful and maddening person to have around. Bursts of creativity, play, and affection alternate with withdrawal and sullen aimlessness. There is no Parent in control. There is no Adult in control. Psychological and social structure is at a minimum. There is a sense of liberation and release that comes from escaping both the strictures of the Parent and the "responsibilities" of the Adult. There is a joy in experiencing once again the wonder, the sense of mystic union with the world, and the unfettered spontaneity of the Child. The "drop-out" mystic truly lets go of the Self—i.e., the Parent Self and the Adult Self. The reward is a return to childhood.

The price of this regression is high. The cost of having a non-functioning Parent is dissipation of psychic energy on trivia. The Parent contains all sorts of data useful for survival. There is a structure of good and bad, safe and dangerous, productive and useless, economical and extravagant. This structure greatly simplifies the decision-making necessary for day-to-day living. When this automatic structure is not operating, then everything is up for grabs, and the decision about whether to stay up all night or get some sleep is as important and as trivial as a decision about getting married or getting laid. The Parent Self can be a tyrant. But it can be a guide for survival as well. Get rid of the Parent, and you get rid of the guide as well as the tyrant. The mystic drop-out, as described by Douglas, is unable to distinguish in the Parent the useful guide from the domineering tyrant. Only the Adult can do this, and the alienated mystic has silenced his Adult as well as his Parent. The rational Adult Self that might have separated the appropriate data from the destructive in the Parent is not functioning. The alienated Child is reduced to the option of accepting or rejecting the whole package. This is one of the costs of retiring from the burdens of Adult responsibility. In surrendering this rational control along with Parental control, the life of the alienated mystic floats along at the mercy of the Child's whims. It is doubtful, of course, that even the most alienated of mystics could turn off completely his Parent and his Adult. The question is one of emphasis. In Douglas' view, mysticism flourishes best in those societies which minimize the structure that comes from both group pressure and individual responsibility, i.e., from Parent and from Adult. In this interpretation, mystical experience is a regression. It is a way of rejecting both social order and self-chosen goals. It is a retreat from social duty and individual responsibility. Again, if the practice of mysticism necessarily leads to this result, it can hardly be urged as a valid human ideal.

These distorted and life-denying varieties of mysticism give some basis for the mystic's poor image in the eyes of the practical man-in-the-street. In the popular mind, the mystic is a social drop-out. And there are mystics who are such. They die to their Parent Self and Adult Self, leaving their Child in control. A Child cannot cope in an Adult world where premium is put on a rational responsible use of power. In the popular mind, the mystic is an ineffectual religious conformist. And there are mystics who revel in this masochistic life-style. They die to their Adult, thereby surrendering all control to their Parent. The resultant rigid life-style is ill-suited to the world of Adult affairs which requires reasonable flexibility for survival. We conclude that the pursuit of mystical enlightenment is a two-edged sword. One needs a wise Master to discern the genuine and life-affirming experience of enlightenment from these inauthentic and destructive varieties. For the genuine mystics the pursuit of enlightenment was a way of fulfillment, a path not to destruction but to true reality. Let's look at the psychological structure of genuine mystical experience.

The genuine mystic, like Douglas' social drop-out, dies to the Parent Self. But the genuine mystic does not die to his Adult. This growth and realization of the Adult Self is precisely what sets authentic mysticism apart from its distorted destructive forms. All the great mystical traditions speak of self-emptying, of letting go of the self. This "letting go," in modern psychological terms, is a liberation from the dogmatic strictures and condemnations of the Parent. The Parent no longer pulls the puppet strings or lashes out with the whip of guilt. More important still is the liberation from the super-Parent, a tyrannical view of God whose infinite clout reinforces the "not-OK" self-image of the Child. Part of mystical ecstasy is the sense of liberated autonomy that results when the Parent dies.

For the social drop-out, the death of the Parent left the spoiled Child in complete control. For the genuine mystic, the passing of the Parent signals the release of the Adult. The Adult through the process of detachment and meditation comes to touch and realize his ultimate reality (in the *tao*, in *nirvana*, in *Brahman*, etc.). With the Parent blocked out and the Adult in control, the natural creative "OK" Child can now experience its own worth. My Child senses that it is accepted absolutely and unconditionally. I am not lovable *provided that* I obey, conform, or get forgiven. No. My natural Child experiences a sense of intimacy and of its own worth with no strings attached. Such is *p'u*, the natural self. Such is my original Buddha-nature. Such, in Christian terms, is grace, unearned because it need not be earned. It is there already and from the beginning. It is only with the Parent and the super-Parent that a sense of worthlessness is introduced and learned. Mystical release from the Parent is a return to original goodness where the intimacy of the "OK" Child is joined with the experience of ultimacy by the Adult, where *p'u* is bathed by *tao*, or *Atman* by *Brahman*, or where the Buddha-nature rests in *nirvana*. In a word, genuine mysticism is life-affirming. It is a path to the self-realization of the Adult and the spontaneous creative Child. The only Self that dies is the Self that is an obstacle to this realization, the Parent and super-Parent that would like to stifle the Adult and fill the Child with guilt. Genuine mysticism is poles apart from masochism. The Child's spontaneity with the Adult's autonomy will have nothing to do with neurotic self-destructive conformity to external forces (the Parent). This is the authentic mystic's answer to Berger. And there is nothing in the genuine mystic that requires him to be an ineffectual social drop-out, a spoiled Child flailing around, *sans* Parent and *sans* Adult. Douglas' drop-out mystic is the epitome of powerlessness. The genuine mystic, liberated from Parental domination, with the Child's creativity released and the autonomous Adult in control, is the very picture of strength. As the Taoist puts it, he is a man of *te*. This power of the genuine mystic is precisely what makes him suspect to the organized prophetic religions. Society and organized religion would have nothing to fear from an alienated social drop-out.

So the first objection brought against mysticism at the beginning of this chapter is really not an objection at all. It is true that the mystic is a poor candidate for becoming a company man. He cannot be trusted to take the rules of the game too seriously. He is a man who lives "beyond good and evil." His behavior will not be confined to the morality of this or that group. His enlightenment, in other words, has detached him from his Parent. So any government or society or religious institution that wants to play Parent over him is not going to succeed. He will not be taken in. His Adult is in charge, not his Parent. He sees through the conventions and rules of any given group. This does not mean he will be a rebel. It is doubtful that an enlightened man would take any group's conventions or dogmas seriously enough to rebel against them. Paradoxically enough, his very detachment may enable him to play the rules of the game more effectively than others who are not so detached. The mystic is strong in his sense of acting from the depths of his true reality.

He does not have the anxieties of those people who are seriously caught up in the need to conform.

"Mystic" is still a derogatory term for most of us in the West. A society, we feel, has little to fear and little to gain from its mystics. This poor reputation is deserved by the distorted forms of mysticism. Society indeed has little to fear from the alienated pseudo-mystics who have dropped out and live at the fringes. A church has little to gain from members who surrender themselves to it in masochistic conformity. They are little more than living stereotypes whose lives are rigidly patterned by the Parent, be it Mother Church or Father God. But a society or a church has much to gain from those genuine mystics who see things as they really are, who are beholden to none but the Absolute Reality, and whose childlike and innocent creativity is secured to an Adult self rooted in the depths of being.

Notes

Chapter I: How To Meditate

[1]Claudio Naranjo and Robert Ornstein, *On the Psychology of Meditation* (New York: The Viking Press, 1971). I have relied heavily in the second, third, and fourth chapters on Naranjo's threefold breakdown of meditation into the way of concentration, the negative way, and the way of surrender.

[2]Maurice Nébdoncelle, *God's Encounter with Man* (New York: Sheed and Ward, 1964).

[3]Joan Baez, *Daybreak* (New York: The Dial Press, 1968).

[4]In two beautifully written books, Dom Aelred Graham has brought Christianity into fruitful encounter with Hinduism and especially with Buddhism. See his *Zen Catholicism* (New York: Harcourt, Brace, and World, Inc., 1963) and *The End of Religion* (New York: Harcourt Brace Jovanovich, Inc., 1971).

[5]From *Alfred Lord Tennyson, A Memoir by His Son* as quoted by Alan Watts in *Does It Matter?* (New York: Vintage Books, 1971), p. 86.

[6]Baez, *op. cit.*, p. 115.

Chapter II: Concentrative Meditation

[1]The teachings of Chuang-Tzu, a Chinese Taoist, will be discussed in the later chapter on Taoism.

[2]The *Vedas* are the Hindu scriptures. See the chapter on Hinduism.

[3]Naranjo, *op. cit.*, pp. 62-63, lists these objects of medita-

tion taken from the fifth-century Buddhist writer, Buddhaghosa.

⁴The *Yoga* system of Patanjali will be outlined in more detail in the chapter on Hinduism. Here we cite the eight steps of *Yoga* merely to show by example how arduous the meditative path really is.

Chapter III: The Negative Way

¹Mt. 5:27-28, Moffat translation.

²From the Buddhist *Dhammapada*, Chapter I, as quoted in Lin Yutang's *The Wisdom of China and India* (New York: Modern Library, 1942), p. 327.

³*The Varieties of Religious Experience* as quoted by Robert de Ropp, *The Master Game: Pathways to Higher Consciousness Beyond the Drug Experience* (New York: Delacorte Press, 1968), pp. 50-51. This excellent book treats mystical experience from every conceivable angle. R. de Ropp elaborates on the doctrine of the five levels of consciousness outlined in this chapter. This ancient teaching has been made known to the modern world chiefly through the work of the Russian mystics Gurdjieff and Ouspensky.

⁴See C. G. Jung's Foreword to Daisetz Taitaro Suzuki's *An Introduction to Zen Buddhism* (London: Rider Press, 1957), pp. 13-14.

⁵Thomas Merton, *New Seeds of Contemplation* (New York: New Directions Edition, 1972), p. 221.

Chapter IV: The Way of Surrender and Self-Expression

¹Thomas Merton, *The Way of Chuang Tzu* (New York: New Directions, 1965), p. 88.

²For the technical foundations of this kind of analysis, see Peter Berger and Thomas Luckmann, *The Social Construc-

tion of Reality: A Treatise in the Sociology of Knowledge (Garden City, New York: Doubleday and Company, Inc., 1966).

Chapter V: Hinduism

[1] For a thorough explanation of Indian philosophy which is at the same time congenial to the English-speaking mind, see Ninian Smart, *Doctrine and Argument in Indian Philosophy* (London: George Allen and Unwin, Ltd., 1964). A little more technical but absolutely superb is Poolla Tirupati Raju's *The Philosophical Traditions of India* (London: George Allen and Unwin, Ltd., 1971).

[2] Alan W. Watts, *The Book: On the Taboo Against Knowing Who You Are* (New York: Collier Books, 1966). See especially Chapter One.

[3] From *The Bhagavad Gita*, Chapter Two, in John B. Alphonso-Karkalo (ed.), *An Anthology of Indian Literature* (Middlesex, England: Penguin Books, Inc., 1971), pp. 114-115.

[4] One of the more lucid explanations of *sankhya* philosophy in its relationship to *Yoga* is contained in *How To Know God: The Yoga Aphorisms of Patanjali*, translated with commentary by Swami Prabhavananda and Christopher Isherwood (New York: Signet Book Edition, 1969).

Chapter VI: Buddhism

[1] Besides the works of Smart, *op. cit.*, and Raju, *op. cit.*, three good books on the life and philosophy of the Buddha are *The Buddhist Tradition in India, China and Japan*, Wm. Theodore de Bary (ed.) (New York: The Modern Library, 1969); Christmas Humphreys, *Buddhism* (Baltimore: Penguin Books, 3rd edition, 1962); and the anthology of texts in *World of the Buddha*, Lucien Stryk (ed.) (Garden City, New York: Anchor Books, 1969).

Chapter VII: Taoism

¹All of these facts can be explored further in the brief, accurate, witty and well-written introduction to Taoism by Holmes Welch, *Taoism: The Parting of the Way* (Boston: Beacon Paperback Edition, 1966).

²Chapter 16 of the *Tao Te Ching* in the translation quoted by Chang Chung-yuan in *Creativity and Taoism: A Study of Chinese Philosophy, Art and Poetry* (New York: Harper Colophon Book, 1970), p. 127.

³Chapter 25 of the *Tao Te Ching* in Arthur Waley's classic translation, *The Way and Its Power* (London, 1934), quoted by Welch, *op. cit.*, p. 53.

⁴*Ibid.*, p. 55, quoting from Chapter 1 of Waley's translation.

⁵An eighth-century Chinese verse translated by Chung-yuan, *op. cit.*, p. 57.

⁶Max Kaltenmark, *Lao Tzu and Taoism* (Stanford: Stanford University Press, 1969), p. 84.

⁷See the Foreword by C. G. Jung to the best English edition of the *I Ching* which is: *The I Ching or Book of Changes*, the Richard Wilhelm translation rendered into English by Carey F. Baynes (Princeton: Princeton University Press, third edition, 1967).

Chapter VIII: Zen

¹See, for example, Daisetz Taitaro Suzuki, *Essays in Zen Buddhism* (3 vols.) (London: Rider Press Edition, 1949, 1950, 1951) and *Introduction to Zen Buddhism* (New York: Philosophical Library, 1949); Alan Watts, *The Way of Zen* (New York: New American Library, 1957) and *Does It Matter?* (New York: Vintage Books, 1968). These are only four among dozens of English language books on Zen by Suzuki and Watts, many in paperbound editions. This author takes issue not with the rich background and obvious scholarship of

these Zen writers, but with the pose that Zen transcends all cultural definitions and forms.

[2]The classic on Zen history translated into several languages is Heinrich Dumoulin, S.J.'s *A History of Zen Buddhism* (New York: Pantheon Books, 1963).

[3]For the introduction to the West of the Zen priesthood with all its doctrine and ritual, see Jiyu Kennett's excellent *Selling Water by the River: A Manual of Zen Training* (New York: Vintage Books, 1972).

[4]Abbot Zenkei Shibayama, *A Flower Does Not Talk: Zen Essays* (Rutland, Vermont: Charles E. Tuttle Company, 1970), pp. 215-16.

[5]Dumoulin, *op. cit.*, p. 236.

[6]*Ibid.*, p. 237.

[7]Nancy Wilson Ross, *The World of Zen* (New York: Random House, 1960), p. 125.

[8]*Ibid.*, p. 120.

[9]Dumoulin, *op. cit.*, p. 239.

Chapter IX: Mysticism or Masochism?

[1]This objection is developed in Peter Berger's *The Precarious Vision: A Sociologist Looks at Social Fictions and Christian Faith* (New York: Doubleday and Company, Inc., 1961).

[2]The hypothesis upon which this conclusion is based is developed in Mary Douglas' *Natural Symbols: Explorations in Cosmology* (London: The Cressett Press, 1970).

[3]Thomas A. Harris, *I'm OK—You're OK: A Practical Guide to Transactional Analysis* (New York: Harper and Row, 1969).